Facing

Novak Djokovic

By Scoop Malinowski

Cover art by Alberto Ramirez Suarez

CONTRIBUTORS

Taylor Dent
Gilles Muller
Diego Schwartzman
Paolo Lorenzi
Brandon Nakashima
ITF Junior
Marton Fucsovics
Andy Roddick
Nick Bollettieri
Ivan Lendl
Conor Niland
Andrey Rublev
Marat Safin
Holger Rune
Rod Laver
Patrick McEnroe
Fred Stolle
Kristof Vliegen
John Isner
Reilly Opelka
Feliciano Lopez
Denis Shapovalov
Tennys Sandgren
Stefanos Tsitsipas
Lenny Jacobskind
Istvan Kaylop
Olga Danilovic
Sebastian Korda
Brian Dabul
Taylor Fritz
Somdev Devvarman
Maxime Cressy
Gene Mayer
Denis Kudla

Danill Medvedev
Ruben Bemelmans
Bettina Bunge
Harry Cicma
Philipp Petszchner
Samir Banerjee
Ray Collins
Boris Becker
Jack Sock
Sam Querrey
Dmitry Tursunov
Chris Evert
Svetlana Kuznetsova
Jerome Kym
Zlatan Ibrahimovic
Wladimir Klitschko
Dominik Hrbaty
John Skelly
Mike Bryan
Ivan Ljubicic
Scott Royce
Andre Agassi
Pete Sampras
Alexander Zverev
Justine Henin
Sander Groen
Nick Kyrgios
Rafael Nadal
Juan Martin Del Potro
Stanislas Wawrinka
Roger Federer
Miguel Seabra
Dr. Aaron Friedrich

The Beginning

The first time I saw the name "Novak Djokovic" was in the 2005 Roland Garros second round results, he won a set from Guillermo Coria 64 26 23 RET. At that time Coria was a lethal clay court player, a favorite to win the Roland Garros title after blowing the championship point in the 2004 final vs. Gaston Gaudio. Djokovic was an unknown eighteen-year-old at this time, ranked outside 100, and to win a set off such an accomplished clay player as Coria was an astounding and alarming result.

There would soon be many more. By the end of 2006, Djokovic was ranked no. 16 in the world. At the end of 2007 he was no. 3. In early 2008 Djokovic won his first Grand Slam in Australia, ending the eleven consecutive Grand Slam stranglehold monopoly of Roger Federer and Rafael Nadal.

In 2011 Djokovic won three of the four Grand Slams and achieved the world no. 1 ranking for the first time. He won three of four in 2015 too. Novak Djokovic was born on May 22, 1987 in Belgrade, Serbia to Srdan and Dijana Djokovic, who operated a fast food establishment and sporting goods store at Mount Kopaonik. A gift of a small mini racquet and foam ball fascinated young Novak and by age six he was registered into a tennis camp run by former Yugoslavian pro and Wimbledon competitor Jelena Gencic at Teniski Klub Partizan. Observing Novak play, Gencic said, "This is the greatest talent I have seen since Monica Seles."

Gencic developed, honed and refined Djokovic's tennis foundation for six years and then decided in September 1999 it would be best for the 12-year-old to train abroad with stronger competition. She contacted Nikola Pilic, a Roland Garros finalist in 1973, and it was arranged that Novak would train at his academy in Germany which he did for the next four years. At fourteen, Novak became a European singles and doubles champion.

As a junior, Djokovic reached the semifinal at Australian Open in 2004 and a world junior ranking of no. 24. Djokovic's first ATP Tour level tournament was at Umag in 2004 - he lost in the round of 32 to Filippo Volandri. In 2005 Djokovic played his first Grand Slam main draw after qualifying, but was defeated in three sets by Marat Safin.

My first time seeing Djokovic play live was his US Open marathon first round match vs. Gael Monfils on a small outer court. I watched the unforgettable fifth set in fascinated awe of the teen talent and drama. With a fully crowded court (including John McEnroe) watching the fifth set, twice Djokovic collapsed after long rallies in the summer afternoon heat, needing extended medical attention. It looked like Novak might actually expire due to a heart attack or retire from the match from exhaustion, that's how physically drained he seemed. But the clever, calculating court marvel would rise up both times to eventually win the match 75 46 76 06 75. A star was born.

After the match I approached Djokovic in the locker room and he was kind enough to do the unscheduled ten-minute Biofile interview (which you can read later in this book). He was friendly, engaging, charming, polite and very likable with a burning desire that made you understand, this kid didn't just "want" to be a champion... he absolutely was going to be a champion...

Djokovic was the outsider from Serbia. He invited himself to the elite ATP party and then conquered it. Then when the establishment conspired to blockade Djokovic from breaking the Grand Slam 21 record at the 2022 Australian Open over his refusal to inject himself with a drug shot, he became a more popular and beloved heroic force all over the world, similar to Muhammad Ali, who refused to be drafted into the Vietnam war and consequently was forced to relinquish his world heavyweight championship title and passport for three years, thus sacrificing three prime years of his career for a conviction he believed in...

The strong always have to be defended against the weak. - Friedrich Nietzsche

Painting is freedom. If you jump, you might fall. But if you're not willing to take the risk of breaking your neck, what good is it? You don't jump at all. You have to wake people up. To revolutionize their way of identifying things. You've got to create images they won't accept. Force them to realize they're living in a pretty queer world. A world's that's not what they think it is. - Pablo Picasso

Novak Djokovic's
20 Grand Slam Titles

2008 Australian Open

F Jo-Wilfried Tsonga   46 64 63 762

SF Roger Federer   75 63 765

QF David Ferrer 60 63 75

R16 Lleyton Hewitt 75 63 63

R32 Sam Querrey 63 61 63

R64 Simone Bolelli 61 62 62

R128 Benjamin Becker 60 62 765

2011 Australian Open

F Andy Murray 64 62 63

SF Roger Federer 763 75 64

QF Tomas Berdych 61 765 61

R16 Nicolas Almagro   63 64 60

R32 Viktor Troicki 62 (RET)

R64 Ivan Dodig 75 678 60 62

R128 Marcel Granollers 61 63 61

2011 Wimbledon

F Rafael Nadal 64 61 16 63

SF Jo-Wilfried Tsonga 764 62 679 63

QF Bernard Tomic 62 36 63 75

R16 Michael Llodra   63 63 63

R32 Marcos Baghdatis64 46 63 64

R64 Kevin Anderson 63 64 62

R128 Jeremy Chardy 64 61 61

2011 US Open

F Rafael Nadal   62 64 673 61

SF Roger Federer 677 46 63 62 75

QF Janko Tipsarevic   762 673 60 30 (RET)

R16 Alexandr Dolgopolov   7614 64 62

R32 Nikolay Davydenko   63 64 62

R64 Carlos Berlocq   60 60 62

R128 Conor Niland 60 51 (RET)

2012 Australian Open

F Rafael Nadal 57 64 62 675 75	
SF Andy Murray	63 36 674 61 75
QF David Ferrer	64 764 61
R16 Lleyton Hewitt	61 63 46 63
R32 Nicolas Mahut	60 61 61
R64 Santiago Giraldo	63 62 61
R128 Paolo Lorenzi	62 60 60

2013 Australian Open

F Andy Murray672 763 63 62
SF David Ferrer 62 62 61
QF Tomas Berdych 61 46 61 64
R16 Stan Wawrinka 16 75 64 675 12-10
R32 Radek Stepanek 64 63 75
R64 Ryan Harrison 61 62 63
R128 Paul-Henri Mathieu 62 64 75

2014 Wimbledon

F Roger Federer 677 64 764 57 64

SF Grigor Dimitrov 64 36 762 767

QF Marin Cilic 61 36 674 62 62

R16 Jo-Wilfried Tsonga   63 64 765

R32 Gilles Simon 64 62 64

R64 Radek Stepanek 64 63 675 765

R128 Andrey Golubev 60 61 64

2015 Australian Open

F Andy Murray765 674 63 60

SF Stan Wawrinka 761 36 64 46 60

QF Milos Raonic 765 64 62

R16 Gilles Muller 64 75 75

R32 Fernando Verdasco   768 63 64

R64 Andrey Kuznetsov 60 61 64

R128 Aljaz Bedene 63 62 64

2015 Wimbledon

F Roger Federer   761 6710 64 63

SF Richard Gasquet 762 64 64

QF Marin Cilic 64 64 64

R16 Kevin Anderson 676 676 61 64 75

R32 Bernard Tomic 63 63 63

R64 Jarkko Nieminen 64 62 63

R128 Philipp Kohlschreiber 64 64 64

2015 US Open

F Roger Federer 64 57 64 64

SF Marin Cilic 60 61 62

QF Feliciano Lopez 61 36 63 762

R16 Roberto Bautista Agut 63 46 64 63

R32 Andreas Seppi 63 75 75

R64 Andreas Haider-Maurer 64 61 62

R128 Joao Souza 61 61 61

2016 Australian Open

F Andy Murray 61 75 763

SF Roger Federer 61 62 36 63

QF Kei Nishikori 63 62 64

R16 Gilles Simon 63 671 64 46 63

R32 Andreas Seppi 61 75 766

R64 Quentin Halys 61 62 763

R128 Hyeon Chung 63 62 64

2016 Roland Garros

F Andy Murray 36 61 62 64

SF Dominic Thiem 62 61 64

QF Tomas Berdych 63 75 63

R16 Roberto Bautista Agut 36 64 61 75

R32 Aljaz Bedene 62 63 63

R64 Steve Darcis 75 63 64

R128 Yen-Hsun Lu 64 61 61

2018 Wimbledon

F Kevin Anderson 62 62 763

SF Rafael Nadal 64 36 769 36 10-8

QF Kei Nishikori 63 36 62 62

R16 Karen Khachanov 64 62 62

R32 Kyle Edmund 46 63 62 64

R64 Horacio Zeballos 61 62 63

R128 Tennys Sandgren 63 61 62

2018 US Open

F Juan Martin del Potro 63 764 63

SF Kei Nishikori 63 64 62

QF John Millman 63 64 64

R16 Joao Sousa   63 64 63

R32 Richard Gasquet 62 63 63

R64 Tennys Sandgren 61 63 672 62

R128 Marton Fucsovics 63 36 64 60

2019 Australian Open

F Rafael Nadal 63 62 63

SF Lucas Pouille 60 62 62

QF Kei Nishikori 61 41 (RET)

R16 Daniil Medvedev 64 675 62 63

R32 Denis Shapovalov 63 64 46 60

R64 Jo-Wilfried Tsonga   63 75 64

R128 Mitchell Krueger 63 62 62

2019 Wimbledon

F Roger Federer 765 16 764 46 13-12

SF Roberto Bautista Agut 62 46 63 62

QF David Goffin 64 60 62

R16 Ugo Humbert 63 62 63

R32 Hubert Hurkacz 75 675 61 64

R64 Denis Kudla 63 62 62

R128 Philipp Kohlschreiber 63 75 63

2020 Australian Open

F Dominic Thiem 64 46 26 63 64

SF Roger Federer 761 64 63

QF Milos Raonic 64 63 761

R16 Diego Schwartzman   63 64 64

R32 Yoshihito Nishioka   63 62 62

R64 Tatsuma Ito 61 64 62

R128 Jan-Lennard Struff 765 62 26 61

2021 Australian Open

F Daniil Medvedev 75 62 62

SF Aslan Karatsev 63 64 62

QF Alexander Zverev 676 62 64 766

R16 Milos Raonic 764 46 61 64

R32 Taylor Fritz 761 64 36 46 62

R64 Frances Tiafoe 63 673 762 63

R128 Jeremy Chardy 63 61 62

2021 Roland Garros

F Stefanos Tsitsipas 676 26 63 62 64

SF Rafael Nadal 36 63 764 62

QF Matteo Berrettini 63 62 675 75

R16 Lorenzo Musetti 677 672 61 60 40 (RET)

R32 Ricardas Berankis 61 64 61

R64 Pablo Cuevas 63 62 64

R128 Tennys Sandgren 62 64 62

2021 Wimbledon

F Matteo Berrettini 674 64 64 63

SF Denis Shapovalov 763 75 75

QF Marton Fucsovics 63 64 64

R16 Cristian Garin 62 64 62

R32 Denis Kudla 64 63 767

R64 Kevin Anderson 63 63 63

R128 Jack Draper 46 61 62 62

FACING
Novak Djokovic

To be the best in the world at anything, you have to
get blood on your hands.

- Philip H. Anselmo

"My thoughts were he wasn't that good."

Taylor Dent: I played a young Novak Djokovic in Hopman Cup 2006. My agent asked me what I thought of him as a player? My thoughts were that he wasn't that good. But he kept on improving, kept on working and pretty soon later he was considered one of the greatest players of all time.

I beat him in singles (61 64) and also me and Lisa Raymond beat him and Ana Ivanovic in mixed doubles (76 62).

Series tied 1-1

2006 Hopman Cup USA vs SER   Outdoor Hard   RR   Dent   61 64
2010 Wimbledon   Outdoor Grass R64   Djokovic 765 61 64

"He makes you suffer on the court."

Gilles Muller: To be honest, I prefer to play Federer than Nadal or Djokovic. Because they make you suffer on the court. They make you physically suffer on the court. And Roger's more the guy who hits winners. So it's not as hard physically to play him.

Djokovic won series 4-0

2016   ATP Masters 1000 Paris Indoor Hard R32   Djokovic 63 64

2016   ATP Masters 1000 Canada Outdoor Hard R32   Djokovic 75 763

2015   Roland Garros   Outdoor Clay R64   Djokovic   61 64 64

2015   Australian Open Outdoor Hard R16 Djokovic   64 75 75

"Everything is difficult."

Diego Schwartzman: Everything is difficult against Novak. I think what he's doing when he's playing his best, he's moving the ball... to every single point on [the] court. It's very difficult to see or to know what he's going to do and [to] try to make good points... He has a lot of talent when he has the chance to move the ball.

Djokovic leads series 6-0

2020	Nitto ATP Finals Indoor Hard RR Djokovic 63 62	
2020	ATP Masters 1000 Rome Outdoor Clay F Djokovic 75 63	
2020	Australian Open Outdoor Hard R16 Djokovic 63 64 64	
2019	ATP Masters 1000 Rome Outdoor Clay SF Djokovic 63 672 63	
2017	Roland Garros Outdoor Clay R32 Djokovic 57 63 36 61 61	
2014	US Open Outdoor Hard R128 Djokovic 61 62 64	

"He's very meticulous, on every shot."

Paolo Lorenzi: My first memory of Novak Djokovic...that's a memory I think was good for him because he beat me easy a few times. I play him on Queens center court, I was playing him in Australia, in New York. I think I have good memories because when I play against him, I know I have to improve a lot of things.

Question: Why and how does Djokovic stand out from other players?

Paolo Lorenzi: I think because he's good in everything. He has very good reaction, he has good serve, he has unbelievable returns, he's moving well, he's attacking good, he's defending good. That's the heel of his game.

Question: When you played Novak, did you have any success against him at all?

Paolo Lorenzi: No. Unfortunately no [smiles].

Question: Is he the toughest guy for you to play?

Paolo Lorenzi: I think they're all very tough to beat. It was really tough to play against him or Rafa, Roger or Andy - the toughest matches. But against him, for me, I think it was really, really tough.

Question: Lasting memory of Novak, on or off court?

Paolo Lorenzi: It's also when he practices. He's very meticulous. He puts very much attention to his shots, ever shot. And I think it's the heel of his game and his success. Really focused on every shot.

Question: Does it make you a better player from having played him?

Paolo Lorenzi: I think having played all the big ones made me a better player. Because you watch them, you know you have to improve a lot of things. When you are with them, you realize you are not so good [smiles].

Djokovic leads series 3-0

2012   US Open Outdoor Hard R128 Djokovic   61 60 61

2012   Australian Open Outdoor Hard R128   Djokovic 62 60 60

2010   London / Queen's Club Outdoor Grass R32   Djokovic 63 63

"Super-focused."

Brandon Nakashima: The biggest thing I've learned from practicing from Novak Djokovic would be just the way he goes about everything. It's how he's super-focused, pays attention to all the little details both on the court when he's practicing and during the matches as well.

"Regular guy."

ITF Junior: I met Djokovic in Miami a couple of years ago and had the chance to hang out with him for a while one night. I got the impression that he was a regular guy and that he preferred it when strangers or fans interacted with him as a normal person, he would be more engaging and naturally friendly. But if someone approached him like a total starstruck fan asking for autographs or selfies, he would oblige them politely but he wouldn't interact or connect with them. I learned it's best to treat a superstar like any other regular person, that is what they prefer.

"I can rally with him."

Marton Fucsovics: Against Novak, against the top guys, there is not really -- you cannot tell the winning strategy. Maybe his game is not so entertaining like Federer's or when Nadal is hitting the ball so hard, and actually, I like to play against him. I can rally with him. I played him three times, he beat me, but I like the way he plays. I think we play the same kind of tennis. We like to rally. We like to play long rallies and try to play aggressive from the baseline. Yeah, he's playing good. Ht puts a lot of balls in the court, not to hit the big winner. He wants me to miss.

Djokovic leads series 4-0

2021	ATP Masters 1000 Paris	Indoor Hard	R32	Djokovic	62 46 63
2021	Wimbledon	Outdoor Grass	QF	Djokovic	63 64 64
2019	Doha	Outdoor Hard	R16	Djokovic	46 64 61
2018	US Open	Outdoor Hard	R128	Djokovic	63 36 64 60

"He beat me like a DRUM."

Andy Roddick: First he takes your legs. Then he takes your soul. Novak in crunch time has become a different animal. I'm not sure if I've ever seen someone at the start of their career, maybe when you counted on them being a little fragile in those moments, maybe you could grind them down physically. The correction that he's made in his career certainly is amplified in a match like the 2019 Wimbledon final (vs. Federer, won 13-12 in the fifth set after saving two championship points). Where he started to where he's gotten to is unlike anything I've seen before from a given player.

Question: What was a very memorable match vs. Djokovic?

Andy Roddick: I remember 2012 at the Olympics. I played Novak second round. I was unseeded but had won a couple of weeks before. I'd won two of the last three tournaments I had played in (Atlanta final vs Gilles Muller and Eastbourne vs. Andreas Seppi). So I was feeling great. I felt like Wimbledon was a place where maybe I could catch lightning in a bottle, make a bit of a run. Felt great in practice that week. I beat (Martin) Klizan in the first round (75 64). Went out in second round - and Novak was someone who I'd had a decent record against, to that point (5-3 career head to head before the match). And he... beat... me... like... a DRUM. I was like a child on the court. I walked off the court - I lost 2 and 2 on grass (actually 2 and 1). I served average. It's not a good thing for me to serve average against Novak. I walked off the court and thought: I'm gonna go out tomorrow and feel like I'm playing well. He just beat me like a drum. That was one of the first times - US Open was a couple of months later - that's when I said to myself, This is getting a little bit different than what I had been used to. These guys are kind of from another planet right now. That one kind of hit home for me. The way he was playing in that moment was eye-opening for me.

Question: Comments after seeing him win the 2021 Roland Garros title?

Andy Roddick: Physically and mentally dominant. Hardest player in history to attack through the court. No holes in his game. No holes physically. Can't break his mental belief. Well deserved.

Roddick won series 5-4

2012   London Olympics Outdoor Grass R32   Djokovic   62 61

2010   ATP Finals Indoor Hard   RR   Djokovic 62 63

2010   ATP Masters 1000 Cincinnati Outdoor Hard QF   Roddick 64 75

2009   ATP Masters 1000 Canada Outdoor Hard QF Roddick 64 764

2009   ATP Masters 1000 Indian Wells Outdoor Hard   QF Roddick 63 62

2009   Australian Open Outdoor Hard QF Roddick 673 64 62 21 RET

2008   US Open Outdoor Hard QF Djokovic 62 63 36 765

2008   Dubai Outdoor Hard SF Roddick   765 63

2007   ATP Masters 1000 Canada Outdoor Hard QF Djokovic 764 64

"Perfect player."

Nick Bollettieri: Djokovic is the most perfect player in the history of tennis. When you look at match players in the history of tennis, I don't believe that anybody can equal everything on the court that Djokovic does. I don't think you can find a weakness in his game. His movement, personality, his return of serve, his serve, excellent touch, not hesitant in coming to the net, great serve. Overall, almost every player has a downfall... to me, he doesn't have one. He's perhaps the best put-together player that I've seen over 60 years.

"Best returner in the world."

Ivan Lendl: If you look at who hits the ball the deepest in the world right now in men's tennis, to me it's Novak. Who returns the deepest in men's tennis - Novak. Who is the best returner in the world - Novak. So the depth has a lot to do with it. I think the depth is what a lot of younger players don't understand or appreciate enough.

"You're on the back foot."

Conor Niland: I was really excited to just test myself against Djokovic at the US Open in 2011 on Arthur Ashe Stadium. He was no. 1 in the world, I qualified for the main draw (ranked 197). I always felt like my groundstrokes were a really high level. My serve wasn't really and my variety and stuff wasn't amazing, but I was really looking forward to getting the chance to just be out there and go toe-to-toe with Djokovic at least within the point.

I just felt like his returns were so good. You're on the back foot on all the returns. His depth...[Djokovic] was able to go up levels. He was probably at a point where if I increased my level by ten percent he would have increased his fifteen anyway. I don't think I experienced him being at his absolute best in that match. I had to retire in the second set due to food poisoning (at 06 15).

Djokovic won series 1-0

2011 US Open Outdoor Hard R128 Djokovic 60 51 RET

"A lesson."

Andrey Rublev: It looks like everything is fine, it looks like I'm playing some good rallies, but then suddenly I'm making so many unusual mistakes, easy, from positions that normally I'm playing well and hitting hard from. I was missing a lot... It means I was rushing too much.

I was rushing a bit, overthinking a bit. Because every time I was thinking 'OK, now I have a chance to attack, now I have a chance to lead the point'. You think through the next two, three, four shots and then in the end you don't even make this one, you know? And normally you just shoot and you don't think.

This is normal, I have to pass through this experience. I've been through this when I was playing my first meeting against Andy (Murray - loss 63 60 62 at 2017 Australian Open R64, but won second meeting at 2021 Rotterdam 75 62), against Rafa (Nadal - loss at 2017 US Open QF 61 62 62 but won third meeting at 2021 Monte Carlo 62 46 62), and it always takes time.

You need to play a couple of matches like this to feel your opponent and feel that you can compete with the best players. It takes time... Now is the time to take a lesson from this match and to give my best for the next match.

Djokovic leads head to head series 1-0

2021 Nitto ATP Finals RR Indoor Hard Djokovic 63 62

"Future top ten."

Marat Safin on Novak match in 2005 at AO: He's a young guy, upcoming. He had a very good results last year in the Challengers. He's going to be a good player. He sign already a few contracts, so that means that the people, they're looking forward and he's going to be in the future Top 10.

Marat on Novak match in 2008 at Wimbledon: if you have a second round against Djokovic, the guy won the Australian Open, semifinals of French Open, winning the tournaments left and right. You play against him, and the last time I won two matches in a row was I don't remember when. So what do you expect? Of course that you are not really in a position to look anything after the second round.

I just had to do what I had to do - serve well and try to stay with him. And also he didn't impress me with his game today. I could read his serve. I could return. I could stay with him from the baseline, and that's it.

Yeah, well, he's a nice guy, a great answerer and great for you guys. I think he scored some points over there by saying that (he lost due to playing badly rather than Safin playing well), yeah, he played well and everything. But he had small chances. He didn't take them. Whenever I had a chance I went for it, and I just played, like I said, solid, took my chances.

Safin won series 2-0

2008 Wimbledon Outdoor Grass R64   Safin   64 763 62
2005 Australian Open   Outdoor Hard   Safin 60 62 61

"Djokovic is the most giving."

Holger Rune: I wrote to him on Instagram. Whether he was in Monaco or in the area - because I had seen that he had withdrawn from Miami. Then he wrote back: 'Hello Holger, yes, we can do it.'

We hit together before - I was his training partner at the 2019 ATP Finals in London.

I've had some experience at this level now and I know the difference isn't that big either. There are some small things, some decisions that you make in different situations, but I think I can at least play with him. I have to move well. He hits the ball so clean. He has such a good meeting point, hardly makes any mistakes. It's just so cool to train with him. You get a good rhythm.

I always feel great emotions when I train with the top 10 because they have so many strengths to draw from and at the same time they are fantastic guys who love tennis like me. I measure my tennis against theirs, I know there is still a lot to improve, but I don't feel that far from their level. When I was training with Djokovic, I realized that he was not only on the tennis court, but also outside is a very strong person: I have an idea why only few can beat him on tour. He's the most complete player I've ever seen, both mentally and physically. Thanks to his advice, I have written down many things that I need to work on. He showed me what it takes to become number one in the world... It's not just about passion or good tennis, there is an immense job behind it.

I think a lot of people have great tennis to get to the top of the rankings, but to break the number one longevity records of Djokovic, Federer and Nadal, you need a little more. I would like to have a career similar to them, it would be fascinating.

Question: What is the best advice that you have received from the 'Big Three?'

Holger Rune: Djokovic asked me the first time I practiced with him - I think I was fourteen years old and I was a hitting partner for him in Monaco - if I liked the way I played tennis. And I said yes. And he said good, that's important.

At that time I thought it was a little strange but later I have thought about it and it is very important to like your tennis. Not only playing tactically or playing what your coach tells you works best, but also playing your own tennis. The tennis that makes ME happy.

Djokovic has told me many good things. It's funny because it's always Federer and Nadal that are mentioned as the good guys but in terms of the future generations, I think Djokovic is the most giving. I haven't heard Federer or Nadal giving too much advice to the young players, maybe they do to the youngsters from their countries. But according to me, Djokovic is the most giving.

Djokovic leads series 1-0

2021 US Open Outdoor Hard R128 Djokovic 61 675 62 61

"He thrives on challenges."

Rod Laver: I'm thrilled for Novak. He likes the challenge that is always there. That's what he thrives on. Not very often does he find himself unable to play his best tennis. He's a different player. Mentally, he's strong. A game or two down in the fifth doesn't mean anything to him. He keeps battling on... A lot of people, including myself, think that Federer is the best ever at the moment. But Novak's compiling a big record, so you've got to look at his career. You have to put him in that group with the greatest players. He has to be up there.

"Most complete player of all time."

Patrick McEnroe: Is Novak Djokovic the greatest player of all time? That's still up for debate. It certainly appears he's on his way, however. What's apparent now is that Djokovic is the most complete player of all time.

"He beat the top guns."

Fred Stolle: Happy for Djokovic. For fourteen years fans cheered for either Nadal or Federer. So when Djokovic started to beat 'their guy' it did not sit too well. Think about it ... Djokovic was no. 3 in the world before starting to beat the 'top guns.'

"He did not know my game and strategy."

Kristof Vliegen: Yes I did play him. First time was in Davis Cup (second round) in 2005 on clay in Belgrade. He was already playing a very high level for his age (17 and ranked 142) at that time but you can't compare that to the level he has now for more than ten years. He was not ready to run to dropshots during Davis Cup. He did not know my game and strategy. I tried to put a lot of energy with my forehand and serve... and to mix up a lot which worked out well that day. I won in four sets (63 63 36 62). Olivier Rochus had beaten Novak in the Friday singles match in five sets (61 57 76 16 36) so Novak lost both singles of that tie.

(Note: Djokovic won his immediate following tournament after the Davis Cup tie vs. Belgium, at the San Remo, Italy Challenger, beating Francesco Aldi in the final 63 76. A week later on May 22, Djokovic turned 18.)

In Dubai in 2007, he was ranked 14 in the world, I was ranked 49. I was a break up in the third set as well... we played on a small court which was an advantage for me I do believe...smaller court gave me always the feeling that the court was faster. This was on hardcourt, the conditions were pretty good after some days of bad weather. I remember in that match that he improved so much his backhand. I could not really hurt him anymore... every point was taking six or seven or eight hits each. He won 46 64 63.

Question: The next two tournaments after you played Djokovic, he excelled - right after your Dubai match he reached the finals of 2007 Indian Wells, losing to Nadal in the final 62 75 and then he won the next tournament Miami Open vs. Canas in the final 63 62 64. In Miami he avenged Nadal in the QF 62 64. (Also in 2007 Novak reached the semifinals of Roland Garros, Wimbledon and the US Open final.) After you beat him in Davis Cup in 2005, he won his very next tournament at San Remo Challenger. So playing you seemed to give Novak some good luck.

Kristof Vliegen: I did not know that. I will ask him for a percentage on his prize money. I will be rich [laughs].

Series tied 1-1

2007   Dubai Outdoor Hard   R32   Djokovic 46 64 63

2005   Serbia vs. BEL 2nd RD Outdoor Clay RR Vliegen 63 63 36 62

"He's the best returner
I've ever faced."

John Isner: He is the best returner I've seen for sure. He is No. 1 and No. 2 and No. 3. He's the best returner I've ever faced. I've said that before, too. So he's a very good tennis player. There are some things tactically I can do better against him on the serve. With him, it's not necessarily   a lot of times he gets the return back with interest, but if he just gets it back, period, no matter how the return is, he's going to be in the point with his defensive skills.

Sometimes he blocks his forehand return on the deuce side. Maybe I could serve and volley a little bit more there, I guess, but, I don't know.

He's No. 1 in the world for a reason. I have to play pretty close to my best to beat him.

To beat Novak or any of the guys that are at the top of the game I have to play very, very solid. I've only beaten him twice, and even that, I think, is a pretty good achievement. He's the No. 1 player in the world. Simply put, he's a better tennis player than me. He just is. His record proves that. But on any given day, I think I can beat anyone.

Question: Lasting memory of Novak on or off court?

John Isner: Nole always has and always will be class. He's an absolute legend in my book that has brought so much good to millions around the world.

Djokovic leads series 10-2

2019 ATP Masters 1000 Shanghai Outdoor Hard   R16 Djokovic 75 63

2018 Nitto ATP Finals Indoor Hard   RR   Djokovic 64 63

2015 Beijing Outdoor Hard   QF Djokovic 62 62

2015 ATP Masters 1000 Miami Outdoor Hard SF   Djokovic   763 62

2015 ATP Masters 1000 Indian Wells Outdoor Hard R16 Djokovic 64 765

2014 ATP Masters 1000 Indian Wells Outdoor Hard SF Djokovic 75 672 61

2013 ATP Masters 1000 Paris Indoor Hard R16 Djokovic 675 61 62

2013 ATP Masters 1000 Cincinnati Outdoor Hard QF Isner 765 36 75

2013 USA vs. SRB WG QF Indoor Hard RR Djokovic 765 62 75

2012 ATP Masters 1000 Indian Wells Outdoor Hard SF Isner 767 36 765

2010 Beijing Outdoor Hard   SF Djokovic   761 62

2010 SRB vs. USA WG 1st RD Indoor Clay   RR Djokovic   75 36 63 676 64

"He did a lot of great things
for the sport."

Reilly Opelka: What's not complicated for Novak is to stay on the training court for an extra hour in 2008, during the Cincinnati Masters, just to sign all the balls of the children waiting for him. I was one of them. He did a lot of great things for our sport...I think well of him.

"No weaknesses."

Feliciano Lopez: When Novak plays good, you don't know what to do to be honest. He has no weaknesses in his game. When Rafa and Roger were at their best they weren't as great as Djokovic is now.

Djokovic leads series 9-1

2017   ATP Masters 1000 Madrid Outdoor Clay R16   Djokovic 64 75

2016   ATP Masters 1000 Indian Wells Outdoor Hard R16 Djokovic 63 63

2016   Dubai   Outdoor Hard QF Lopez 63 RET

2015   ATP Masters 1000 Shanghai Outdoor Hard R16 Djokovic 62 63

2015   US Open   Outdoor Hard QF   Djokovic 61 36 63 762

2012   ATP Masters 1000 Shanghai Outdoor Hard R16 Djokovic 63 63

2011   Belgrade Outdoor Clay F   Djokovic 764 62

2011   Dubai   Outdoor Hard   R16   Djokovic 63 26 64

2007   ATP Masters 1000 Miami Outdoor Hard R16   Djokovic 60 63

2007   Australian Open Outdoor Hard R64   Djokovic 62 75 61

"I have tremendous respect for him."

Denis Shapovalov: He came up to me in the locker room (after our Wimbledon semifinal 2021 76 75 76). Ge said a couple words. Told me he knows how difficult it is for me right now but that it will all come. For me it's big coming from someone like him. It was awesome to hear those words from him. He doesn't have to do it, it's very nice from him to do it. It shows what kind of guy he is. He isn't praised enough. I have tremendous respect for him. He's an incredible guy.

He does a really good job of putting pressure when it's needed. And you feel it exactly in those moments and he steps up. He does that really well.

I felt like I was outplaying him from the back a good portion of the match. And if you can outplay Novak you can beat anyone in the world.

Djokovic leads series 7-0

2021	Wimbledon Outdoor Grass SF Djokovic 763 75 75
2021	ATP Cup Australia Outdoor Hard RR Djokovic 75 75
2020	ATP Cup Australia Outdoor Hard QF Djokovic 46 61 764
2019	ATP Masters 1000 Paris Indoor Hard F Djokovic 63 64
2019	ATP Masters 1000 Shanghai Outdoor Hard R32 Djokovic 63 63
2019	ATP Masters 1000 Rome Outdoor Clay R32 Djokovic 61 63
2019	Australian Open Outdoor Hard R32 Djokovic 63 64 46 60

"It is impossible to surprise him."

Tennys Sandgren: Djokovic is the best ever. We do one thing and he does another. We try to hit a winner, while he places the ball in difficult areas, where it is impossible to surprise him. He suffocates you slowly. What he does is just incredible.

I have a lot of support for Novak. I personally find him to be a great inspiration, not just from a tennis perspective but also how he carries himself, watching how he fights through the things he's going through. How he goes about his training and how meticulous he is, the work ethic he puts into it. I want to see him win. I want to see him play, I want to see him compete. I want to see the drama. I know there's gonna be a lot of drama. At the end of the day, we love that about sports.

Djokovic leads series 4-0

2021   Roland Garros Outdoor Clay R128   Djokovic 62 64 62

2020   ATP Masters 1000 Cincinnati Outdoor Hard R16 Djokovic 62 64

2018   US Open   Outdoor Hard R64 Djokovic 61 63 672 62

2018   Wimbledon Outdoor Grass R128Djokovic 63 61 62

"Almost perfection."

Stefanos Tsitsipas: For sure he has almost reached perfection, Novak, in his game style, the way he plays, which is unbelievable to see, honestly. That inspires me a lot to go out and work and try to reach that perfection, that ability to have everything on the court.

I feel happy and at the same time sad. Could have been a better result for me today. Novak showed once again what an incredible athlete [he is] and his ability on the courts. [It] was difficult, for sure, playing him. I think [he is] one of the most difficult opponents I've faced in my entire life. I have huge respect for that. He gave me a really difficult time on the court.

Question: When did you first meet Djokovic?

Stefanos Tsitsipas: I met Novak Djokovic for the first time in Monte Carlo in 2008. I was still small, first came to Monaco. I left with a photo with Novak. My father told him that one day we would meet on the court. Then it sounded crazy, but it turned out that he was right. The photo I have somewhere, I am sure that I can find it.

Djokovic leads series 6-2

2021	Roland Garros	Outdoor Clay	F	Djokovic	676 26 63 62 64
2021	ATP Masters 1000 Rome	Outdoor Clay	QF	Djokovic	46 75 75

2020   Roland Garros   Outdoor Clay SF   Djokovic   63 62 57 46 61

2020   Dubai   Outdoor Hard   F Djokovic   63 64

2019   ATP Masters 1000 Paris Indoor Hard   QF Djokovic   61 62

2019   ATP Masters 1000 Shanghai Outdoor Hard QF   Tsitsipas 36 75 63

2019   ATP Masters 1000 Madrid Outdoor Clay F   Djokovic 63 64

2018   ATP Masters 1000 Canada Outdoor Hard R16 Tsitsipas 63 675 63

"Novak helped a
spectator propose to his girlfriend."

Lenny Jacobskind: One time at the Miami Open some years back a spectator asked Novak after practice if he could help him propose engagement to his girlfriend and he did. I thought that was cool of him. She said Yes, fortunately [laughs]. Novak happens to be one of the nicest guys with fans and very generous with autographs now and before he started winning Grand Slams. I believe his antics on the court at times are mild compared to some of the players in the 1980's and before when they were able to say and do almost anything. All of us tennis fans are used to the mild-mannered Federer and Rafa but Novak gets irritated more quickly. I may be in the few out there, but I like all the big three.

"Happy, fun, good guy."

Istvan Kaylop: I have met Novak several times and as we all know tennis is a sport with extremely cool and kind, fan-friendly players as a whole. Novak, is by far and beyond, one of the nicest, kindest and most appreciative pro tennis players you will ever come across. Such a happy, fun and good guy.

"He inspires you to be better."

Olga Danilovic: He's no. 1 for me in every part of being a tennis player. When you talk to him, you think, Okay, now I'm going to beat everyone after talking to him. His energy and dedication and his passion to play and work is something that pushes inspires you to be better.

"I watched him at US Open
when I was nine."

Sebastian Korda: I watched Radek Stepanek play Novak Djokovic in Ashe Stadium at US Open when I was nine years old (from player box as his dad Petr was coaching Stepanek at the time). That's when I realized I wanted to be a professional tennis player, not a hockey player.

"He greets me with a hug."

Brian Dabul: A nice anecdote at Roland Garros about ten years ago. I lost in the first round to Janko Tipsarevic (67 16 06) remember it was the second week of Roland Garros (2011) and I decided to stay and train in Paris before my next tournament in Europe (Rijeka, Croatia Challenger). In the tournament office I put in a request to train with any player. A few hours later I went to the court to see if they managed to find anybody for me to hit with. And for one of those reasons only fate knows, I ran into Novak Djokovic and his entire work team. Nole agreed to train with me a day before his (third round) match with Juan Martin Del Potro. In the practice we played a soccer tennis match with his fitness coach and physical therapist and then trained for a little over an hour. What surprised me most was the ease and timing that he struck the ball while standing literally above the baseline. During that training, Nole must have failed on only three balls. At the end I asked for a photograph to keep it as a memory. After that day, every time we crossed paths he greets me with a hug and talks to me about Diego Maradona, one of his childhood idols. A great among great, Novak Djokovic, the best tennis player of the last decade. My admiration and respect for this tremendous champion.

"Novak is Novak."

Taylor Fritz: The biggest memories for my first two matches with Novak, especially Monte Carlo, it was windy and it was hard for me to pinpoint my spots. I had to play with more margin, and that's definitely not something I can get away with when I'm playing him.

Madrid, a bit of altitude, a bit faster, I was able to attack more and play more aggressive and had a bit of a closer match. I just know what to expect and I know what I need to do.

For me to have a chance to beat Novak, I just have to play my best tennis. Luckily for me and my game, I possess the ability if I'm on, I can serve well enough to where I won't get broken and I can be extremely aggressive on the ground strokes and I can kind of take control if I'm on.

In Australian Open (2021 third round loss 76 64 36 46 62) he was serving unbelievable in the fifth set. He was serving two first serves and barely really missing any, hitting the spots, serving faster, harder than he was before in the previous sets. I found it even tougher to return his serve.

Then much more pressured, as well, to hit a better return because he was stepping in and just cracking it so well and not missing. He was making some mistakes, some errors in the third and fourth, and just cracking the ball and not really missing in the fifth. I didn't feel like I really had a good chance.
And then he was also just putting a lot of pressure on my serve with how he

was attacking it. He was picking a side, and if he guessed the right side he just, like, just crushed the return.

That was tough to deal with and it was also obviously tough to deal with him all of a sudden moving fast and just like playing so much better from the third and the fourth. I mean, I should have -- I expected that. But I expected that if he was really, really injured he wouldn't The grand scheme of things, I need to keep working, I need to get everything better. I need to get, like, my serve, for the first set and set and a half, it wasn't where it should have been for me. I was serving like 50-something percent and not hitting my spots. I was making too many forehand mistakes when I was trying to be the aggressor in the rallies.

And I've improved my movement a lot, but I have to keep working. I have to keep improving. You know, it's very motivating that we're so close, we're so close.

But also, at the same time so far these guys are so good. I definitely got a taste for why Novak is Novak in the first-set tiebreaker. These guys are so good. I have a lot of work to do.

Question: Your comments on the mental strength factor of Novak? The roaring, screaming, fist pumps in key dramatic moments of the fifth set of the AO match?

Taylor Fritz: I think a lot of it is just, like, the desire and the passion and wanting it, and I don't think it's something that these guys develop. I think it's something that you're born with. They're just kind of -- they're built differently. I think that I want it, I think I want it just as bad, and I have the passion and desire just as much, but I still need to develop my game so I can show it. It doesn't matter how bad you want it if you're not better than the other person.

So I think these guys have just, like, they just want it. Like I said, they are kind of just built differently, and it's something that people have or they don't have, and it makes, that's what makes someone a champion.

Djokovic leads series 5-0

2021   ATP Masters 1000 Paris Indoor Hard   QF Djokovic 64 63

2021   ATP Masters 1000 Rome Outdoor Clay R32 Djokovic 63 765

2021   Australian Open Outdoor Hard R32 Djokovic   761 64 36 46 62

2019   ATP Masters 1000 Madrid Outdoor Clay   R32   Djokovic 64 62

2019   ATP Masters 1000 Monte Carlo Outdoor Clay   R16 Djokovic 63 60

"He said to me, Just to let you know, you can win this match."

Somdev Devvarman: The best match I played against the top four of Federer, Djokovic, Nadal and Murray was against Rafa in Indian Wells in 2011, fourth round. I played three really good matches before that, I beat Baghdatis, Malisse. So then I played Rafa. Before the match while I was stretching and warming up I remember Novak came up to me and he said, 'Just to let you know, you can win this match, right? I was like, Okay. He looked at me, 'Also to let you know, he has one of the worst backhands on the Tour.' And Rafa was no. 1 in the world at the time! I played really well in that match. I played more to his backhand. I lost 75 64. I think it shows the mindset of these top guys when they play each other. They see weaknesses and then they let them try to beat them with their weakness. I think when Djokovic goes out to play Rafa, a part of him really believes Rafa has a bad backhand. And he can beat him going to that side. I think that's the point to take away from this.

Djokovic won series 1-0

2013 ATP Masters 1000 Miami   Outdoor Hard   R32   Djokovic 62 64

"Really fun guy."

Maxime Cressy: When I was in Monte Carlo I met Djokovic. Really fun guy. I was training in Monte Carlo and I saw him, he was training there. And I saw him. He was with his wife and dog. I was eight. I got an autograph. He was like early 20s, taking off on the ATP Tour.

"Very solid in a learned way."

Gene Mayer: I met Djokovic countless times, up until recently. I was playing the seniors at all the Grand Slams except for Australia. He knew me and the rest of the "legends."

Question: Technically Djokovic is an excellent player, like you were known as a technically sound player. Does his technique remind you of you in any way?

Gene Mayer: Not really me. He's very solid in a learned way without a lot of improvisation.

Question: Do you think he would be an even better player if he had more "improvisation"? How could he develop that aspect?

Gene Mayer: That would potentially change his whole approach to the game. Not sure that is doable or advisable at this stage of his career.

"He could be the greatest athlete of all time."

Denis Kudla: I think he's the greatest of all time. I think he will surpass all of the records by a lot when all is said and done. He just plays the game so incredibly well. It would have been interesting to see if the ages were a little different, if Fed was the youngest, or Rafa was the youngest. I think Novak deserves to be the greatest of all time. He is the greatest of all time. He does things nobody is willing to do. I don't think he's just the greatest of all time in tennis. He could be the greatest athlete of all time.

Djokovic leads series 3-0

2021   Wimbledon Outdoor Grass   R32   Djokovic 64 63 767

2019   US Open Outdoor Hard R32 Djokovic 63 64 62

2019   Wimbledon Outdoor Grass R64 Djokovic 63 62 62

"He doesn't miss."

Daniil Medvedev: I like to play against Novak. We have, since the first one when I was ranked 60, we had always tough matches physically, mentally. And he's one of the greatest tennis players in the history of tennis.

When Novak says he's not gonna hand anything to somebody, I believe him. I'm not gonna say I don't trust him. I trust him. So I know that to beat him you need to just show your best tennis, be at your best physically maybe four or five hours, and be at your best mentally maybe for five hours. Never know how the match is going to go.

I would say to win a slam, especially against somebody as Novak, is already a big motivation, and I don't think there is anything that can make it bigger. I like Novak. I appreciate him as a tennis player. And I should say as a person. To be honest, I think it's when he's in the zone he doesn't miss. He goes down the line, cross, forehand, backhand, he doesn't miss. That's what is the most, the toughest part of playing against him.

So that's why some matches that we played are really I think unbelievable matches. I find them -- you know, few times I saw the highlights, and I was, like, Wow, this level is unbelievable.

The first time I play with Novak... I don't remember the year. Probably I was going to Minsk, to Belarus, for Futures. He was going to Montreal, Toronto, I don't remember which one of the two, after just winning Wimbledon. It was my coach, I think talk to top players, he just said he wanted to hit with somebody in Monaco, I was around.

I come there to hit with Novak, also hearing stories in the media that Novak is not a nice guy, all this. He was late. That's the only bad thing I remember, that he was late (smiling). He was super nice to me. I was really shy. I was like, you know, staying just playing some balls, trying not to miss, for sure really stressed. I'm playing the world No. 1 and all this. He was super nice. Nothing much to say.

After that experience we had some other stories where he took me on a private jet to Serbia on Davis Cup. Still I was just two weeks in the top hundred or something like this. Yeah, he was always really nice to me. He helped me a lot I would say for my confidence in my career.

I play Nadal and Djokovic in my first two Grand Slam finals US Open and Australian Open. Was two different matches, for sure. Just they play differently. One is a lefty, the other is a right handed, straightaway. And Rafa gives you more time to think on the court. But then, you know, he's amazing in defense. He's amazing with his forehand. You feel like you won the point, he makes some crazy shots. But you have time to think and you have time to adapt to things. With Novak, I felt like I wanted to mix up things, I wanted to try to do something different, but I felt like he took all the time from me, he took all the advantage in his side straightaway.

I rank Novak in top three hardest opponents that I ever faced. I'm not joking. I mean, I played all of them. I think when they want to - is not a good word - I'm sure they want to win every tournament also, but when they're in the zone, and I'm not shy to say it, I feel like they're just better tennis players, again, which shows facts and numbers, than the rest of us.

For sure, when we are also in the zone, we can bring them big fight, we can win some matches, some maybe big titles. But it's just that the percentage is on their side. Yeah, I rank Novak in these top three toughest opponents in my life.
I think for sure it is his determination, but not only against the young guys.

I think it would be the same if he would be playing Roger or Rafa. Before a match, we always talk tactics before the match with my coach, the day before. Usually takes five, ten minutes, some small things. Probably where I'm going to serve, what I'm going to do during the points.

When it's against Novak, it took like probably thirty minutes. Why? Because we played already, like, I don't know, maybe seven matches before this one, maybe even more. Every match was different just because he's so good that every match is different. He changes his tactics, he changes his approach. What was different before Australian Open (2021) that I had, yeah, clear plan in my mind what I have to do in which moment. Of course, it would depend a lot on him because, again, sometimes you have to be aggressive, sometimes defensive. I had a clear plan which did seem to work.

Was he at his best in the US Open final? Maybe not. He had a lot of pressure. I had a lot of pressure, too, about the risk on the second serve, it was because of the confidence I had. I knew I cannot give him easy serves because that's what he likes. So that was the plan. Because of the confidence in a lot of tight moments, I managed to do it well.

I did beat him once in straight sets. Was in London. I think tennis is such brutal sport where there is no room for error when you're playing top guys. I am a top guy; he is a top guy. London can be the same. I went out of the match in Nitto Finals, and I was like, That was strange, it was easy.

I guess, it's all together. Maybe he had a bad day. If we talk about Australia, I definitely didn't play my best there. But, again, probably people are going to say, Well, Novak destroyed him, whatever.

It's always about the small details. Again, he definitely was not at his best. We saw him playing better. The question is, if he would be (at his best), would I be able to keep up with him? We can never know now. I'm just happy to win (smiling).

Djokovic leads series 6-4

2021	ATP Masters 1000 Paris Indoor Hard F Djokovic 46 63 63	
2021	US Open Outdoor Hard F Medvedev 64 64 64	
2021	Australian Open Outdoor Hard F Djokovic 75 62 62	
2020	Nitto ATP Finals Indoor Hard RR Medvedev 63 63	
2020	ATP Cup Outdoor Hard SF Djokovic 61 57 64	
2019	ATP Masters 1000 Cincinnati Outdoor Hard SF Medvedev 36 63 63	
2019	ATP Masters 1000 Monte Carlo Outdoor Clay QF Medvedev 63 46 62	
2019	Australian Open Outdoor Hard R16 Djokovic 64 675 62 63	
2017	Eastbourne Outdoor Grass SF Djokovic 64 64	
2017	SRB vs. RUS WG 1st RD Indoor Hard RR Djokovic 36 64 61 10 RET	

"It's like he was in your mind."

Ruben Bemelmans: Yes I played Novak in Hopman Cup. I was playing alongside Justine Henin against Djokovic and Ana Ivanovic. In singles it's like playing against a wall. He's so quick, his defensive skills are unbelievable. The ball keeps coming back. I remember then he was not playing as powerful as Federer or Nadal. He was like all over the court. It was like he was in your mind and he knew what you were gonna do. It's just amazing how he was reading the game and bringing back the balls. With enough quality as well, so I couldn't do much. It feels like you're just playing against a wall.

Question: Lasting memory of Novak on or off the court?

Ruben Bemelmans: Now, recently, I don't know if you're aware of it...there's a player union created, PTPA. He's backing it. That shows that he cares about the future of tennis and the lower ranked players. I think it's a great thing from him. It shows that he really cares about the sport, also for the lower ranked players, that they should have a better life or better earnings in the sport.

Djokovic leads series 1-0

2011 Hopman Cup SER vs Bel Outdoor Hard   Djokovic 63 62

"It would depress me if he lost a big match."

Bettina Bunge: I saw Novak's dark side. I was numb. Especially after being such a supporter, to the point that it would depress me if he lost a big match. I was floored, but at the same time glad I saw the light... No one was there, except me. It was during the women's final, he had the day off. No one knew he was there, otherwise it would have attracted a lot of people. I was chatting with the guy he was hitting with, this Portuguese low ranked player. I went up to him, since there was not one soul besides him and me there. He was waiting for Novak. We were talking nicely, Novak and team came up, and Novak didn't even greet me. I simply said "Hi", I do that with everyone! He was just an ass, especially to his team. Yelling at them, treated them like slaves. And he seemed so angry. After seeing that I can't stand him now.

"He makes you feel like you're his good friend."

Harry Cicma: As a reporter and TV news anchor (in New York City for NBC and Miami for CBS) , whenever I have communicated with Novak in person, he always makes you feel like you're his good friend. It is ironic that he is so gifted at making people feel comfortable in person, but he doesn't project that as well on the grand stage in front of an audience. I think it's symbolic of how the best tennis players know how to go into the zone during competition, and turn it off after the match. Novak's success comes from his powerful mind.

"I felt like I had a chance."

Philipp Petzschner: Andy Murray was the hardest one for me to play of the Big Four, Federer, Nadal, Djokovic and Murray. Against the others I was able to change the tempo and the rhythm of the point. Against Djokovic, I had a tough match at US Open first round, first match of the night session. I think it was 57 67 46. I played a lot of slice backhands. With my slice I could take a little bit of the speed out of the point. Then with the forehand I kind of could change it up. I had a pretty fast forehand but I could also play it slow and heavy. So against Djokovic, when I went slice against his backhand, he couldn't do much. Or it felt like he couldn't do as much. I didn't beat him but I felt like I had a chance at least. So I felt like I was kind of there. Most likely, pretty far away [smiles]. Against Andy, whatever I did, he did better. So the moment I played fast, he played faster. The moment I played slow, he played slower. Or it's always like I tried to mix it up and somehow he screwed me over with it [smiles]. I played Andy twice but it was more like the practice lessons than the real matches that I played. He beat me 62 64 in Doha (2009).

Djokovic won series 1-0

2010   US Open Outdoor Hard R64 Djokovic 75 63 766

"It's so effortless the way he hits."

Samir Banerjee: I was very fortunate to be a hitting partner (duties shared with fellow ITF junior Jerome Kym) for all the players at the ATP Nitto World Tour Finals in Turin, Italy (2021). At the US Open, a representative from the ATP talked to my parents about the opportunity (Banerjee won 2021 Boys Wimbledon and finished his ITF junior career ranked no. 3). The ATP said, we'll pay for everything, just come to Italy... all expenses paid, just come train with us, learn about the ATP, what goes on behind the scenes, learn how the players prepare. So it's really a cool program that they're doing.

Definitely nervous before my first hit with Medvedev, definitely my first hit with Djokovic, I was pretty tight. I didn't make as many balls as I would have liked. I think practicing with Djokovic was just crazy, because it's so effortless the way he hits and it just comes, Boom, boom. And Medvedev hits so flat it barely bounces on those courts, it comes so fast. It definitely took a lot of adjustments. It was a tough ball to deal with at first, especially indoors, but I got the hang of it, so it was good.

I posted a video of me playing with Djokovic. I won a point and my friends are like, Djokovic has nothing on you. Just fun stuff. I don't think they knew I was going, so it was pretty funny.

The biggest thing I learned was preparation before matches ... those guys are in the gym an hour to 45 minutes before with their team, just doing different dynamic stuff, working up to full warmup stuff. It's a lot more than you see on court—the preparation that goes into it, the cool down that goes after. It's a lot of moving pieces, and I think if I can incorporate some of that off-court stuff into my game, it will definitely help me.

©Henk Abbink

"Novak was unable to run down my volley-lob."

Ray Collins: I was a travel writer for a Sarasota, FL-based magazine called Family Beautiful. I had been working with the public relations department of the Ritz Carlton Key Biscayne for a feature article. I told them I'd be on the Key to watch the nearby Miami Open. They invited me to take part in a Pro-Am event early in the tournament as one of the members of the media who would play a point with the pros. I was to play with Andy Murray - against Novak Djokovic and Ana Ivanovic [smiles]. Hall of Famer Cliff Drysdale was Master of Ceremonies. After he introduced me, I approached by designated partner but before I could say my name he said, 'Hi, I'm Andy Murray.' With the accent it sounded more like ONDY Murray. I chuckled at his modesty and manners. I said, 'Ha ha, yes, I know you, I'm Ray Collins.' He might have smiled and nodded and I went to my position to receive serve from the No. 1 player in the world Novak Djokovic. Novak laid in an easy serve and a long rally began that lasted about 23 hits. I later saw on the video tape that my new best friend Andy guarded his head for my first few groundstrokes, not being sure if I had ever played tennis before (Ray played NCAA Division 1 at St. Bonaventure University). As the point progressed and the four of us were having a rat-a-tat-tat volley at the net, Novak hit a couple of volleys to my forehand before catching me flat-footed on a hit to my backhand. Out of desperation, I put the racquet behind my back and luckily - and that's the understatement of all time - managed to 'volley-lob' the ball over the head of the man with winning head to head records vs. Roger Federer and Rafael Nadal. Novak attempted to run down the ball and hit a tweener but was unable to track it down. I quickly went over to Andy, we laughed together, slapped a high-five, and I said, 'Did I just do that?' 'Nice shot, mate!' he said with a smile in his voice. Noval and Ana were equally excited for my good luck and off I went to start my Fifteen Minutes of Fame. The video of the shot has been viewed over 45,000 times on You Tube under "Ray Collins Trick Shot."

"Numbers don't lie."

Boris Becker: Numbers don't lie. The number of weeks at No. 1 is very important. Novak is simply way ahead there. If the Big 3 stopped playing tennis today, I would see Novak at No 1.

"He's a really good guy, funny, upbeat, serious."

Jack Sock Interview I did at 2010 US Open:
World No. 3 Novak Djokovic has used American Jack Sock as a frequent hitting partner during the 2010 U.S. Open and the teenager from Lincoln, Nebraska talks about his unique experience and perspective of the charismatic and colorful former Australian Open champion who will take on Roger Federer in Saturday's semifinal...

Question: How did you get the opportunity to hit with such an accomplished player as Novak Djokovic?

Jack Sock: It was before his first night match here (vs. Philipp Petzschner in second round). And I was still here (after losing first round in main draw vs. Marco Chiudinelli 16 46 61 16). He just needed a warmup before his night match and I was still around and I went out around the P courts and just warmed him up. I guess I did a pretty good job and he played a guy that hit a lot of slices, so he asked me to hit a lot of slices. So I hit like twenty in a row. And he was probably happy with me. So his coaches got in contact with my coach and asked me to actually come out to this private court in New Jersey (private residence court in Alpine in Bergen County) about twenty minutes away. To go out and hit there. I did that two days later. And then I warmed him up again before the next time he played (vs. James Blake) around here. Then I went back to his private court again, the next day to practice again with him. We had some pretty good

73

hits together and just spending a little time together. I was just trying to do my best out there and make as many balls as I can in the warmups that I had with him.

Question: Did he talk with you and talk about tennis?

Jack Sock: On the changeovers we talked about our paths growing up, just the basic stuff.

Question: We know he's a character with a great sense of humor, did you see that at all in the practices?

Jack Sock: He's funny in practice too. Once in a while, out of nowhere he'll do a really loud, funny grunt that makes you laugh. He's a really good guy, upbeat and he's a pretty funny guy. But on the day he warms up before a match, he's different. Very serious. It's very strict and routine. He doesn't really talk to anybody.

Question: Did he offer any advice to you?

Jack Sock: He kind of just said I've been doing pretty well lately, he just said to keep doing what you're doing, obviously your coach knows what he's doing. You guys have made a good run lately and throughout my junior career - it's been pretty good. He thinks we know what we're doing, so keep doing what you're doing, then you'll get better, you'll be at this level someday. That was inspirational.

Question: Was there anything that surprised you about Djokovic?

Jack Sock: Not really. I heard he's a funny guy, seeing all his imitations and stuff. I knew he's probably a little jokester here and there. Not really. The way he plays, how clean he hits the ball is pretty amazing. I mean, obviously they're all incredible - the top five in the world - but the level is just crazy.

Question: Do you think Djokovic can win the tournament?

Jack Sock: Oh yeah. I think anybody left can win on any given day. Beat the other guy on any given day. Obviously, Nadal and Federer are going to be a really tough out, they're playing pretty well, Nadal is always a fighter and doesn't miss. But I mean, they're all going to be a tough out. It's gonna be a great weekend of tennis.

Djokovic lead series 1-0

2015   ATP Masters 1000 Canada Outdoor Hard R16 Djokovic 62 61

"He beat me nine other times."

Sam Querrey: My most memorable match with Djokovic was beating him at Wimbledon (76 61 36 76. Unbelievable win. He beat me nine other times, that's the only one I can remember [smiles]. It's definitely the biggest win I've ever had. It's not career defining, but it's really exciting. It's something that I'll always get to have, which is great.

Question: What happened that day?

Sam Querrey: I just won more points than him [smiles]. Served well the whole time. Played a great tiebreaker at the end to get the win.

Question: Multiple rain delays a factor?

Sam Querrey: It was tricky. I think we went on and off four times, including the two sets the first day. So it made it tricky the second day. I think going out I lost the first four games, and I think the rain delay helped me. I got to regroup. I broke back once in the third set which helped me gain back a little momentum for the fourth set. Like I said, with that rain delay, made a couple adjustments, came back out. Kind of settled down a little bit. Lost the third set, but played well the last four games of it. The fourth set was similar to the first set. I was saving a lot of breakpoints early. Every game I held, it put a little more pressure back on him and a little less on me.

Question: When did you realize you could beat the ATP world no. 1 Novak Djokovic that day?

Sam Querrey: I'm not going to lie and say going into it I thought I was going to win. But I think as the match progressed, I was serving well and holding in the first set, we were kind of going back and forth, I gained a little more confidence with every game. We got to that tiebreaker and I played a great tiebreaker. Once I won that, I was like in my head, All right, I can beat this guy, I can hang with him and turn this into a match.

He's played at such a high level for so long. What makes him so good is he wins those matches where he isn't playing his best. Definitely in the second set, yeah, he lost some momentum. He wasn't playing like he usually does. He made me earn it. He's not a guy that goes away. He made me come out and win those big points. Probably not the best he's ever played, but not the worst he's ever played. He was No. 1 in the world and the best out there.

Question: Remember what advices your coach (Craig Boynton) gave you vs Novak?

Sam Querrey: Craig did an unbelievable job. We had been working together all year. He also was coaching Steve Johnson. Every time we were going on and off, he just kept things very simple for me, Throw the ball up on the serve, pick a target, hit it. Don't think about it. Keep thinking about your second serve, return of serve. Make sure you're always smiling out there, having fun. I got to have him in my ear a lot because we had so many rain delays. He kept reminding me of that, which was helpful.

Question: Before beating Novak at Wimbledon you had beat him before in Paris Bercy. Did it help you at Wimbledon to beat Novak?

Sam Querrey: I think it helps. I didn't really pick anything from that match or recollect anything specific from that match. The fact I had one win gave me a little bit of belief like, Hey, maybe I can do it again. I also had eight losses going into it. But, yeah, it definitely helps to have the one win under my belt.

Djokovic leads series 9-2

2019   ATP Masters 1000 Cincinnati Outdoor Hard R32 Djokovic 75 61

2016   Wimbledon Outdoor Grass R32   Querrey 766 61 36 765

2014   US Open Outdoor Hard R32 Djokovic 63 62 62

2013   Beijing Outdoor Hard QF Djokovic 61 62

2013   USA vs. SRB WG QF Indoor Hard RR Djokovic 75 674 61 60

2013   ATP Masters 1000 Indian Wells Outdoor Hard R16 Djokovic 60 766

2012   ATP Masters 1000 Paris Indoor Hard R32 Querrey 06 765 64

2012   ATP Masters 1000 Canada Outdoor Hard R16 Djokovic 64 64

2010   SRB vs. USA WG 1st RD Indoor Clay RR Djokovic 62 764 26 63

2008   ATP Masters 1000 Monte Carlo Outdoor Clay QF Djokovic 64 60

2008   Australian Open Outdoor Hard R32 Djokovic 63 61 63

"He can abuse Rafa's backhand."

Dmitry Tursunov: Novak is able to use his weapons against Rafa better than anybody else. He knows how to play him better than anybody else. Djokovic is able to neutralize his spin by taking the ball early, by sort of absorbing that attack that Rafa can generate. And then just sort of able to slingshot it back. He plays much better positioning against Rafa than anybody else. Like Roger gets thrown off by Rafa quite a bit. Because Rafa's got too much power for Roger. He can kind of sit on his backhand a little bit and just start abusing it. But Novak kind of does that to Rafa. He is able to neutralize his weapons and he knows him so well. A lot of times it's tough for Rafa to come up with something extra. His game patterns are so ingrained. He's not going to serve and volley. And to let Novak just figure it out.

Djokovic won series 1-0

2008   ATP Masters 1000 Paris Indoor Hard R32   Djokovic 62 43 RET

"Celebrate his greatness."

Chris Evert: I like Novak. He's human. He's smart. He's evolved and thoughtful about improving the sport for players. He gives back to his country. He admits his shortcomings. He has passion. He's not afraid to get into the trenches... Let's start to celebrate his greatness.

"I don't see how to beat him."

Svetlana Kuznetsova

At the Miami Open in 2016 I asked Sveta this question: All the men seem to have no idea how to beat Djokovic. You watch him. Do you see any ideas or ways to solve the almost impossible puzzle about how to beat Djokovic?

SVETLANA KUZNETSOVA: I've been watching yesterday the match of Berdych. For example, Berdych, he was close for me. Last night he was really close some moments, but he had so much pressure in his head to play unbelievable.

They have to play close on the limits, because Novak is every match, he plays just good enough to beat. His level is extremely high every match. What other players, they struggle with their level. When they come to play Djokovic they have so much pressure and so much in the head that it's Novak and he plays good that they struggle.

I think before Rafa was the same when guy come on the court and see Rafa. They're scared. They know they're going to lose. They have no chance. Now they have it with Novak. It's mental, but Novak is extremely fit and plays really well.

I don't see how to beat him from my side, but I'm a girl. I play different sport probably, different game.

"Novak gave me some advice for my serve."

Jerome Kym: To play with the eight best players in the world as a hitting partner at the 2021 Nitto ATP Finals, there is nothing more special than to play with those guys. I'm really happy that the ATP gave me this chance to know a new world. They go to practice to learn new things, on every ball they have a discussion about what they did wrong and what they can do better. Novak Djokovic also gave me some advice for my serve, what I can do better on the second serve. He told me that with [speed] it's easier for him to get the ball back deep in the court. He told me to try two or three times in the game where the ball needs to bounce high, because then he needs to play over his shoulder. I have time to prepare for the next shot and then that will make my game easier.

"Anger brings out his best."

Zlatan Ibrahimovic: When Nole plays and gets angry, anger he brings out his best. And that's how I feel alive. He's a complete athlete. Nole is like me.

"Super Positive Energy."

Wladimir Klitschko: I met Novak at a Miami Heat NBA game in 2013. I don't know if Djokovic is a Klitschko fan, but I'm his for sure! Very cool guy with a good super positive energy!

"He always did a lot for the players."

Dominik Hrbaty: I have the best experience with Novak Djokovic. By the way, out of the big three, he is by far the most popular among other players. Because he always did a lot for the others. When someone needs to stand up, he is in the front line.

I think Novak's coach Marian Vajda is one of the least appreciated coaches in history. He did an enormous work with Novak. They split with each other for a year and when Marian was there again, Novak played at his best. Vajda is the key to make Djokovic emotionally balanced and totally focused on court. If I continued my career and I had the chance to hire Vajda, I would immediately hire him. He would be at the top on the list of coaches. He develops great tactics and from the beginning of their co-operation, Djokovic fixed many things. You can tell that it was Vajda's credit.

Series tied 1-1

2008   SVK vs. SRB WG Play-offs Indoor Hard RR Djokovic 62 64 63

2004   Bratislava CH Indoor Carpet R16 Hrbaty 64 75

"Novak said, 'Hook it up!'"

John Skelly: My last interaction with Djokovic was at a player party in Miami when I was coaching Vince Spadea. Vince and I were unofficial scouts for Ford Models and they wanted some tennis players. I was at valet and standing next to Djokovic and I said, 'Bro, I can get you a modeling contract with Ford Models!' Novak said, 'Hook it up!' But I never pursued it. He was an up and comer at the time. I don't know what year it was but Robin Thicke was at the player party playing his new song (Blurred Lines in 2013). Anyway, we got Jan-Michael Gambill a $250,000 contract with Ford Models but it never worked out. When they had jobs for him, he was traveling on the Tour, when he was free, they had no jobs for him.

"He took the mic and jammed with us."

Mike Bryan: When we recorded our first single record most of the ATP players mocked and ridiculed us except for Novak. He supported what we were doing in music. He even took the stage with us and took the mic and jammed with us when we performed at a player party.

"I never really felt a chance against Roger or Novak."

Ivan Ljubicic: I felt that against Rafa if you do play well you do have a chance which I never really felt against Roger or Novak. I felt like Roger had many, many ways to stop my game. Novak was I think the best returner in the game. By far. He was the only player, not only returning my serves a lot but very well. And that was always the big problem for me being the big server. I just felt Roger had so many ways to win the point. And I always felt that whatever I dropped at him, whatever I threw at him, he found a way to deal with it. He's definitely the most creative player that I ever played against.

Novak was different. You can't beat Novak only with a serve, but it does help you a lot if you can get a lot of free points off that shot.
Novak's tactic is consistency. He beat me five times in a row, that was his tactic and it worked out pretty well. When I beat him in Indian Wells I felt physically much better and I was striking the ball quite nicely, so I was not the one rushing to finish the points off.

Djokovic won series 7-2

2010   ATP Masters 1000 Shanghai Outdoor Hard R32 Djokovic 63 63

2010   CRO vs. SRB WG QF Indoor Hard RR   Djokovic   763 64 61

2010   ATP Masters 1000 Indian Wells Outdoor Hard   R16   Ljubicic 75 63

2010   Dubai   Outdoor Hard   QF Djokovic 26 64 60

2009   US Open   Outdoor Hard R128 Djokovic 63 61 63

2009   ATP Masters 1000 Cincinnati Outdoor Hard R32 Djokovic 765 64

2009   ATP Masters 1000 Madrid   QF Djokovic 64 64

2008   ATP Masters 1000 Monte Carlo   Outdoor Clay   R32 Djokovic 63 63

2006   Zagreb   Indoor Carpet SF   Ljubicic 676 63 64

"Novak did the coolest thing."

Scott Royce: I have never seen him do anything more than glare at the ball kids - and that is when he was glaring at everyone. I became a fan some years ago when at the Australian Open the heat was unbearable and at a changeover, the ball kid prepared the bench for Djokovic and instead of sitting down, Djokovic instead implored the kid to sit whereby Djokovic handed him a towel and a water, grabbed one for himself and sat next to the kid putting his arm around the kid's shoulders, I thought it was the coolest thing and have been a fan since.

"He'll appreciate it more as he gets older."

Pete Sampras: Seven years (as ATP year-end No. 1), for him, I'm sure he sees it as a bonus to all the majors that he's won. But I think he'll appreciate it more as he gets older. He did it at a time where he dominated two of the greats, in Roger and Rafa, and he handled the next generation of players very well – all at the same time. I do think what Novak's done over the past ten years, winning the majors, being consistent, finishing No. 1 for seven years, to me it's a clear sign that he is the greatest of all time.

"He needs ownership over his own process."

Andre Agassi: I never faced Djokovic and I do not want to! I played against Federer and Nadal and that's enough. If you gave me his game, the hardest part about winning this tournament would be going to sleep at night. Because I'd be so excited to come here tomorrow to play...

On coaching Novak: I'm shocked what a fast learner he is. I think his learning curves could be quicker but they have to be his. He's just that kind of guy – he needs ownership over his own process. So if he's not having the energy or the strength, that's something he'll figure out on his own. I've always believed in strength training, I've always believed in eating a healthy range and a quantity of protein. But for years, he did it his own way. You get to a point where if you're not part of the solution you're part of the problem. We agreed to disagree far too often for me to feel like I was helping him, and I cared too much about him to just watch him go through something I felt I could help him with.

"Nobody should be respected more than Novak."

Alexander Zverev: It's always interesting and close when we play each other, so I'm always expecting another tough one... There's always a lot of long rallies, we will run a lot more and suffer, in a way, a lot more as well. I think every single match we have played has been close. We've needed to be at our best and one or two points decided the matches...Ihave to say one thing. Because, for me, there's nobody in the world that should be respected more than Novak, in my opinion. Where he's come from, what he's achieved, he's the greatest player of all time. And I think people forget that sometimes. I think everybody should appreciate that for once.

Djokovic leads series 7-4

2021	Nitto ATP Finals	Indoor Hard	SF	Zverev	764 46 63
2021	US Open	Outdoor Hard	SF	Djokovic	46 62 64 46 62
2021	Tokyo Olympics	Outdoor Hard	SF	Zverev	16 63 61
2021	ATP Cup	Outdoor Hard	RR	Djokovic	673 62 75
2021	Australian Open		QF	Djokovic	676 62 64 766
2020	Nitto ATP Finals	Indoor Hard	RR	Djokovic	63 764
2019	Roland Garros	Outdoor Clay	QF	Djokovic	75 62 62
2018	Nitto ATP Finals	Indoor Hard	F	Zverev	64 63
2018	Nitto ATP Finals	Indoor Hard	RR	Djokovic	64 61
2018	ATP Masters 1000 Shanghai	Outdoor Hard	SF	Djokovic	62 61
2017	ATP Masters 1000 Rome	Outdoor Clay	F	Zverev	64 6

"It bought tears to my eyes, honestly."

Justine Henin: I don't think enough credit is given to him for everything he's done, everything he's accomplished. I don't always agree with his behaviour because, in the end, by trying and wanting to do so well, by wanting to be liked, finally, he goes a little against his nature. This is what people can reproach him for. It is a lack of genuineness also at certain times. And there, he gives us access to a real moment of authenticity.

I know what I felt, at least at that moment, I know what it is to build a shell [around yourself]. I think there are a lot of players who go through that who can understand that. And then all of a sudden you get the sight of it breaking down. That really gave me shivers. It really brought tears to my eyes, honestly. I found that it was there where the armour was falling off.

And that, from perhaps the greatest champion in the history of tennis... to see that humanity at that moment, I thought it was really something beautiful. And all of a sudden, finally, the score didn't matter much and the Calendar Slam didn't matter so much. And that's really what I felt in that moment.

"He won the tournament on fast carpet playing from the baseline."

Sander Groen: I was supposed to play Djokovic in the second round of qualifying for Aachen Challenger but I lost the round before to Alexander Flock. Djokovic qualified and won the tournament. On fast carpet, playing from the baseline which was quite rare back then. I think it was 2004.

(Then 17-year old Djokovic was ranked 242 going into that tournament in November 2004 and rolled through the draw... 1R Stan Wawrinka 62 63; 2R Dick Norman 76 46 63; QF George Bastl 64 62; SF Noam Okun 63 61; F Lars Bergsmuller 64 36 64.)

"He said, 'I'll be open to help."

Nick Kyrgios: I remember Novak was actually one of the only players, when I was young, that came towards me and said, 'If you ever need anything, feel free to reach out and I'll be open to help.' We used to practice a lot together at events. And we continued to practice together in Rome. I forgot my practice shoes one day in Rome and ended up playing in Air Force Ones and actually beat him in a set. He's helped Australia as well. Like during the bushfires, he was supportive, he was helping us out. We are so quick to forget. I feel like the media is so quick to forget. Or so quick to jump on things like this and forget he's actually helped us, like he's reached out. He didn't have to do that. I don't forget that. Most athletes wouldn't do that. Most athletes wouldn't do that. They're selfish. Most athletes are.

Kyrgios leads series 2-0

2017   ATP Masters 1000 Indian Wells Outdoor HardR16   Kyrgios 64 763
2017   Acapulco Outdoor Hard QF Kyrgios 769 75

"Play perfect every moment to beat him."

Rafael Nadal: I think he's very complete player. You have Novak in front and you say, How I can beat him? You know, the backhand is fantastic, the forehand is fantastic, the serve he's doing really well, the movements are probably the best of the world today. The only way to beat him is believe in the victory, play aggressive, and play every moment perfect. So that's what I have to try. My approach to the match is always the same: Try my best in every moment and try to play my game very well. He's a machine.

Djokovic leads series 30-28

2021	Roland Garros	Outdoor Clay	SF	Djokovic	36 63 764 62
2021	ATP Masters 1000 Rome	Outdoor Clay	F	Nadal	75 16 63
2020	Roland Garros	Outdoor Clay	F	Nadal	60 62 75
2020	ATP Cup	Outdoor Hard	F	Djokovic	62 764
2019	ATP Masters 1000 Rome	Outdoor Clay	F	Nadal	60 46 61
2019	Australian Open	Outdoor Hard	F	Djokovic	63 62 63
2018	Wimbledon	Outdoor Grass	SF	Djokovic	64 36 769 36 108
2018	ATP Masters 1000 Rome	Outdoor Clay	SF	Nadal	764 63
2017	ATP Masters 1000 Madrid	Outdoor Clay	SF	Nadal	62 64
2016	ATP Masters 1000 Rome	Outdoor Clay	QF	Djokovic	75 764
2016	ATP Masters 1000 Indian Wells	Outdoor Hard	SF	Djokovic	765 62
2016	Doha	Outdoor Hard	F	Djokovic	61 62
2015	ATP Finals	Indoor Hard	SF	Djokovic	63 63

2015   Beijing   Outdoor Hard F   Djokovic 62 62

2015   Roland Garros Outdoor clay QF Djokovic 75 63 61

2015   ATP Masters 1000 Monte Carlo Outdoor Clay SF Djokovic 63 63

2014   Roland Garros Outdoor Clay F Nadal 36 75 62 64

2014   ATP Masters 1000 Rome Outdoor Clay F Djokovic 46 63 63

2014   ATP Masters 1000 Miami Outdoor Hard F Djokovic 63 63

2013   ATP Finals Indoor Hard F Djokovic 63 64

2013   Beijing Outdoor Hard F Djokovic 63 64

2013   US Open Outdoor Hard F Nadal 62 36 64 61

2013   ATP Masters 1000 Canada Outdoor Hard SF   Nadal 64 36 762

2013   Roland Garros Outdoor Clay SF Nadal 64 36 61 673 97

2013   ATP Masters 1000 Monte Carlo Outdoor Clay F Djokovic 62 761

2012   Roland Garros   Outdoor Clay F Nadal 64 63 26 75

2012   ATP Masters 1000 Rome   Outdoor Clay F Nadal 75 63

2012   ATP Masters 1000 Monte Carlo Outdoor Clay F Nadal 63 61

2012   Australian Open   Outdoor Hard F Djokovic 57 64 62 675 75

2011   US Open   Outdoor Hard F Djokovic 62 64 673 61

2011   Wimbledon   Outdoor Grass F Djokovic 64 61 16 63

2011   ATP Masters 1000 Rome Outdoor Clay F Djokovic 64 64

2011   ATP Masters 1000 Madrid Outdoor Clay F Djokovic 75 64

2011   ATP Masters 1000 Miami Outdoor Hard F Djokovic 46 63 764

2011   ATP Masters 1000 Indian Wells Outdoor Hard   F Djokovic 46 63 62

2010   ATP Finals Indoor Hard RR   Nadal 75 62

2010   US Open   Outdoor Hard F Nadal 64 57 64 62

2009   ATP Finals Indoor Hard RR Djokovic 765 63

2009   ATP Masters 1000 Paris Indoor Hard SF Djokovic 62 63

2009   ATP Masters 1000 Cincinnati Outdoor Hard SF Djokovic 61 64

2009   ATP Masters 1000 Madrid Outdoor Clay SF Nadal 36 765 769

2009   ATP Masters 1000 Rome Outdoor Clay F   Nadal 762 62

2009   ATP Masters 1000 Monte Carlo Outdoor Clay F Nadal 63 26 61

2009   ESP vs. SRB WG 1R Outdoor Clay RR Nadal 64 64 61

2008   Beijing Olympics Outdoor Hard SF Nadal 64 16 64

2008   ATP Masters 1000 Cincinnati Outdoor Hard SF Djokovic 61 75

2008   London / Queen's Club Outdoor Grass F Nadal 766 75

2008   Roland Garros Outdoor Clay SF Nadal 64 62 763

2008   ATP Masters 1000 Hamburg Outdoor Clay SF Nadal 75 26 62

2008   ATP Masters 1000 Indian Wells Outdoor Hard SF Djokovic 63 62

2007   Tennis Masters Cup Indoor Hard RR Nadal 64 64

2007   ATP Masters 1000 Canada Outdoor Hard SF Djokovic 75 63

2007   Wimbledon Outdoor Grass SF Nadal 36 61 41 RET

2007   Roland Garros Outdoor Clay SF Nadal 75 64 62

2007   ATP Masters 1000 Rome Outdoor Clay QF Nadal 62 63

2007   ATP Masters 1000 Miami Outdoor Hard QF Djokovic 63 64

2007   ATP Masters 1000 Indian Wells Outdoor Hard F Nadal 62 75

2006   Roland Garros Outdoor Clay QF Nadal 64 64 RET

"We are close friends."

Juan Martin Del Potro: Well, it's a difficult match to play Novak because we are close friends. For sure we both want to win. Is a big challenge to take these major tournaments (from) them. But also I think we are proud to be close to these legends. I've been during all my career learning with Novak, Roger, Rafa, seeing them winning these events very often. It's amazing. I don't feel sad that I couldn't win Grand Slams because of them. I am just one of the guys that have lucky to be in the same era as them, and it's great. Novak is too fast. His defense are pretty good. When you have chances against the top guys, and you couldn't make it, then they take advantage of the game. It's really difficult to beat a player like Novak.

Really difficult to beat a player like Novak.

He has a great team working with him. Hopefully him, Rafa, Roger is still fighting for Grand Slam, because is so nice to watch them fighting for the history. We just do what we can against them. But Novak has everything to make records in this sport.

Djokovic leads series 16-4

2019   ATP Masters 1000 Rome Outdoor Clay QF Djokovic 46 766 64
2018   US Open Outdoor Hard F Djokovic 63 764 63

2017	ATP Masters 1000 Rome Outdoor Clay QF Djokovic 61 64
2017	ATP Masters 1000 Indian Wells Outdoor Hard R32 Djokovic 75 46 61
2017	Acapulco Outdoor HardR16 Djokovic 46 64 64
2016	Rio Olympics Outdoor Hard R64 Del Potro 764 762
2013	ATP Finals Indoor Hard RR Djokovic 63 36 63
2013	ATP Masters 1000 Shanghai Outdoor Hard F Djokovic 61 36 763
2013	Wimbledon Outdoor Grass SF Djokovic 75 46 762 676 63
2013	ATP Masters 1000 Indian Wells Outdoor Hard SF Del Potro 46 64 64
2013	Dubai Outdoor Hard SF Djokovic 63 764
2012	ATP Finals Indoor Hard SF Djokovic 46 63 62
2012	US Open Outdoor Hard QF Djokovic 62 763 64
2012	ATP Masters 1000 Cincinnati Outdoor Hard SF Djokovic 63 62
2012	London Olympics Outdoor Grass Bronze Del Potro 75 64
2011	SRB vs. ARG WG SF Indoor HardRR Del Potro 76 30 RET
2011	Roland Garros Outdoor Clay R32 Djokovic 63 36 63 62
2009	ATP Masters 1000 Rome Outdoor Clay QF Djokovic 63 64
2008	Tennis Masters Cup Indoor Hard RR Djokovic 75 63
2007	US Open Outdoor Hard R32 Djokovic 61 63 64

"You have to almost enjoy to suffer."

Stanislas Wawrinka: Novak he's a beast mentally. He's gonna stay there. He's gonna push you. Normally he always find solution. He's No. 1 player. He won so many title, so many trophy, and it's always the biggest challenge to play against him.

The secret is simple: I have to play my best tennis, my best game. He's the No. 1 player, amazing fighter, amazing player, but I have enough confidence in myself that when I play my best level I can beat him. But it's the biggest challenge. When you play Novak, the No. 1 player in the final of Grand Slam, it's the biggest challenge you can have.

He knows also that I can play my best tennis in the final of Grand Slam. But, again, now, when you play Novak, even playing your best tennis you can also lose.

I think a little bit of the style of how we play. I think the matchup always been interesting to see because the way we are playing. I'm trying to be aggressive. I can play really hard. He is amazing defender.

I think he's so good that he always find a way to be better. For sure he made me better. That's for sure. Because that's the player I played that well in crazy match in the Grand Slam the first time. And not only him, but the big four, for sure. They made me better. The fact that I tried practice always with them, tried to see what they are doing.

My goal is to push myself until the limit where I can go to be the better player I want. I can. With them, every time I step on the court, even if they are way better in their career, I always have something I need to tell myself. Maybe I can beat them. You need to find a way. If you lose, it's okay. You go back to practice.

That's what happened with them. I saw so many players not even thinking they can beat them when they step on the court. I always try to believe in something, that maybe one day I can beat them, and that's what happened.

But there is no secret. If you want to beat the No. 1 player in the world, you have to give everything. You have to accept to suffer and you have almost to enjoy to suffer.

Djokovic leads series 19-6

2019	US Open Outdoor Hard R16 Wawrinka 64 75 21 RET
2016	US Open Outdoor Hard F Stan Wawrinka 671 64 75 63
2015	ATP Masters 1000 Paris Indoor Hard SF Djokovic 63 36 60
2015	ATP Masters 1000 Cincinnati Outdoor Hard QF Djokovic 64 61
2015	Roland Garros Outdoor Clay F Wawrinka 46 64 63 64
2015	Australian Open Outdoor Hard SF Djokovic 761 36 64 46 60
2014	ATP Finals Indoor Hard RR Djokovic 63 60
2014	Australian Open Outdoor Hard QF Wawrinka 26 64 62 36 97
2013	ATP Finals Indoor Hard SF Djokovic 63 63
2013	ATP Masters 1000 Paris Indoor Hard QF Djokovic 61 64
2013	US Open Outdoor Hard SF Djokovic 26 764 36 63 64
2013	Australian Open Outdoor Hard R16 Djokovic 16 75 64 675 1210
2012	US Open Outdoor Hard R16 Djokovic 64 61 31 RET
2012	ATP Masters 1000 Madrid Outdoor Clay R16 Djokovic 765 64
2011	ATP Masters 1000 Rome Outdoor Clay R16 Djokovic 64 61
2010	ATP Masters 1000 Monte Carlo Outdoor Clay R16 Djokovic 64 64
2009	Basel Indoor Hard QF Djokovic 36 765 62
2009	ATP Masters 1000 Monte Carlo Outdoor Clay SF Djokovic 46 61 63

2009	ATP Masters 1000 Indian Wells Outdoor Hard R16 Djokovic 767 766
2008	ATP Masters 1000 Rome Outdoor Clay F Djokovic 46 63 63
2008	ATP Masters 1000 Indian Wells Outdoor Hard QF Djokovic 765 62
2007	Vienna Indoor Hard F Djokovic 64 60
2006	Vienna Indoor Hard R16 Wawrinka 63 63
2006	SUI v. Ser WG PO Indoor Hard RR Djokovic 64 36 26 763 64
2006	Umag Outdoor Clay F Wawrinka 66 RET

"No secrets out there."

Roger Federer: It's pretty straightforward. I think when we do play against each other it's always exciting. We have great rallies against each other. I like playing against him because it's a battle of the baseline a bit, if you like. It's a challenge right now in the men's game. That's what I like, who I like to play against. Like I said, it's always a great matchup between the two of us. We've played many times. So there are no real secrets out there.

I play him with a lot of slices. He handles that one very well time and time again. He's able to go down and make sure he sets himself up nicely and puts himself in position. He gives away very little unforced errors. You got to push him to do those. If you can't, then you have to play aggressive yourself.

He's just really consistent. Seems like there are not many guys that can hang with him, don't have the tools or dare to go forward, or they aren't daring to serve and volley against him because he's so good on the return. Which he is. He's perfected his game on the hard courts, no doubt about it. He was always a great clay-court player, and because he moves as well as he does, he's solid and consistent now on the grass.

To say the least, it's very impressive. He's having unbelievable career. I think everybody knows that he knows that, as well.

Djokovic leads series 27-23

2020   Australian Open Outdoor Hard SF Djokovic 761 64 63

2019   Nitto ATP Finals Indoor Hard RR Federer 64 63

2019   Wimbledon Outdoor Grass F Djokovic 765 16 764 46 1312

2018   ATP Masters 1000 Paris Indoor Hard SF Djokovic 766 57 763

2018   ATP Masters 1000 Cincinnati Outdoor Hard F Djokovic 64 64

2016   Australian Open Outdoor Hard SF Djokovic 61 62 36 63

2015   ATP Finals Indoor Hard F Djokovic 63 64

2015   ATP Finals Indoor Hard RR Federer 75 62

2015   US Open Outdoor Hard F Djokovic 64 57 64 64

2015   ATP Masters 1000 Cincinnati Outdoor Hard F Federer 761 63

2015   Wimbledon Outdoor Grass F Djokovic 761 6710 64 63

2015   ATP Masters 1000 Rome Outdoor Clay F Djokovic 64 63

2015   ATP Masters 1000 Indian Wells Outdoor Hard F Djokovic 63 675 62

2015   Dubai Outdoor Hard F Federer 63 75

2014   ATP Finals Indoor Hard F Djokovic W/O

2014   ATP Masters 1000 Shanghai Outdoor Hard SF Federer 64 64

2014   Wimbledon Outdoor Grass F Djokovic 677 64 764 57 64

2014   ATP Masters 1000 Monte Carlo Outdoor Clay SF Federer 75 62

2014   ATP Masters 1000 Indian Wells Outdoor Hard F Djokovic 36 63 763

2014   Dubai Outdoor Hard   SF Federer 36 63 62

2013   ATP Finals Indoor Hard RR Djokovic 64 672 62

2013   ATP Masters 1000 Paris Indoor Hard SF Djokovic 46 63 62

2012   ATP Finals Indoor Hard F Djokovic 766 75

2012   ATP Masters 1000 Cincinnati Outdoor Hard   F Federer 60 767

2012   Wimbledon Outdoor Grass SF Federer 63 36 64 63

2012   Roland Garros Outdoor Clay SF Djokovic 64 75 63

2012   ATP Masters 1000 Rome Outdoor Clay SF Djokovic 62 764

2011   US Open   Outdoor Hard SF   Djokovic 677 46 63 62 75

2011   Roland Garros   Outdoor Clay SF   Federer 765 63 36 765

2011   ATP Masters 1000 Indian Wells Outdoor Hard SF Djokovic 63 36 62

2011   Dubai Outdoor Hard F Djokovic   63 63

2011   Australian Open Outdoor Hard SF Djokovic 763 75 64

2010   ATP Finals Indoor Hard SF Federer 61 64

2010   Basel   Indoor Hard F Federer 64 36 61

2010   ATP Masters 1000 Shanghai Outdoor Hard   SF   Federer 75 64

2010   US Open   Outdoor Hard SF   Djokovic 57 61 57 62 75

2010   ATP Masters 1000 Canada Outdoor Hard SF   Federer 61 36 75

2009   Basel   Indoor Hard F Djokovic 64 46 62

2009   US Open   Outdoor Hard SF Federer   763 75 75

2009   ATP Masters 1000 Cincinnati Outdoor Hard   F Federer 61 75

2009   ATP Masters 1000 Rome Outdoor Clay SF Djokovic   46 63 63

2009   ATP Masters 1000 Miami Outdoor Hard SF   Djokovic 36 62 63

2008   US Open   Outdoor Hard SF   Roger Federer 63 57 75 62

2008   ATP Masters 1000 Monte Carlo Outdoor Clay SF Federer 63 32 RET

2008   Australian Open Outdoor Hard SF Novak Djokovic   75 63 765

2007   US Open   Outdoor Hard F Federer 764 762 64

2007   ATP Masters 1000 Canada   Outdoor Hard F Djokovic 762 26 762

2007   Dubai   Outdoor Hard QF Federer 63 676 63

2007   Australian Open Outdoor Hard R16 Federer 62 75 63

2006   SUI v. SER WG PO Indoor Hard RR Federer 63 62 63

2006   ATP Masters 1000 Monte Carlo Outdoor Clay R64 Federer 63 26 63

DJOKOVIC/R. Federer US Open semifinal 2011 Press Conference

6-7, 4-6, 6-3, 6-2, 7-5

THE MODERATOR: Questions, please.

Q. This must hurt, Roger. Can you tell us what your feelings are now and where you think it slipped away?

ROGER FEDERER: Well, I mean, it's awkward having to explain this loss because I feel like I should be doing the other press conference. But it's what it is, you know, I mean.

Yeah, I mean, it's the obvious, really. He came back; he played well. I didn't play so well at the very end. Sure, it's disappointing, but I have only myself to blame, you know.

Q. You seemed like you were taking control in the fifth set. How disappointing is it to not be able to kinda keep that momentum going? You certainly had it in that fifth set.

ROGER FEDERER: Yeah, I had it. There's no more I could do. Snaps one shot, and then the whole thing changes. It's strange how it goes, you know, but it was a good tournament for me.

Sure, I'd love to be in the finals and give myself a chance to win the title, which is not the case now. So I have to accept that and move on.

Q. You just said I have no one to blame but yourself. Where do you lay the blame?

ROGER FEDERER: Maybe I said.

Q. Do you find it amazing that he can come up with two blinding forehands in successive years on match point? The odds are pretty remote, aren't they, of him doing that twice?

ROGER FEDERER: Look, it happens sometimes. That's why we all watch sports, isn't it? Because we don't know the outcome and everybody has a chance, and until the very moment it can still turn. That's what we love about the sport, but it's also very cruel and tough sometimes.
It got me today. It hurts, but it's fine. Could be worse. It could be a final.

Q. Could you hit a much better serve for the return he hit that winner?

ROGER FEDERER: Yeah, much better. I didn't hit the best serve. But it's just the way he returns that. It's just not -- a guy who believes much, you know, anymore in winning. Then to lose against someone like that, it's very disappointing, because you feel like he was mentally out of it already. Just gets the lucky shot at the end, and off you go.

Q. What did he do better this time than when you played in the French Open?

ROGER FEDERER: Are you serious? I mean, I thought it was a close match. I should have won here. French Open was very close, too. He could have won that. It's just one of those matches, you know. I mean, I set it all up perfect, but I couldn't finish it.

Q. What did you see of Novak's reaction and playing to the crowd after he hit that forehand winner? What were you thinking at that point?

ROGER FEDERER: Yeah, I see probably 2% of what he does or other players do because I am focused on my stuff, and I don't look what they're doing. I don't really care. As long as it's sportsmanship, I don't care. I don't know what he did, so it's not an issue.

Q. When a guy hits a shot like that forehand on match point, is that a function of luck, of risk, or is it a function of confidence that someone would make kind of...

ROGER FEDERER: Confidence? Are you kidding me? I mean, please.
Look, some players grow up and play like that. I remember losing junior matches. Just being down 5-2 in the third, and they all just start slapping shots. It all goes in for some reason, because that's the kind of way they grew up playing when they were down.

I never played that way. I believe in hard work's gonna pay off kinda thing, because early on maybe I didn't always work at my hardest. So for me, this is very hard to understand how can you play a shot like that on match point.
But, look, maybe he's been doing it for 20 years, so for him it was very normal. You've got to ask him.

Q. Comparing this loss to the Tsonga loss in Wimbledon being up two sets, how do you react to that? Are you more frustrated with this one?

ROGER FEDERER: Same thing. I felt like I played okay today. Maybe better at Wimbledon, but then again, it's a different surface, it's different opponents.
Today I clearly felt like I never should have lost, where in Wimbledon it was - I don't want to say it was more out of my control, you know - but it's, you know, a bit of reaction tennis on grass. I was never up a break in the third, fourth, or fifth at Wimbledon, which today I was.

I was one serve away, really. Yeah, I mean, I get over these losses quickly. Wimbledon didn't get me down.

Q. You were really dominant until the first game of the third set, and you made quite a few errors in that game. Kinda let him back in the match. Given how much longer it went and all the things that happened, how important or unimportant was that game?

ROGER FEDERER: You have to figure that Novak was gonna get his teeth into the match at one stage, right? It's a pity that it happened then, because I think I had a couple of game points, too. So it hurts getting broken that way.
You know, if it goes 15-40 and you never really have a chance to close it out, it's more acceptable. So like this, it was a bit -- again, a bit unfortunate, I thought. He played well. I didn't serve my very best. It was a combination of many things.

And then what he does really well this year, he front runs really well and he started playing great. It was hard to counter his playing. That's why it was very important to push for the two sets to love lead.

Everything I did today I thought was the right way. He just played really well in the third and the fourth.

Q. After the shot that everyone's talking about, double match point, your next serve was right into his body and he fought it off. That was a good serve, right?

ROGER FEDERER: It was a better serve. I don't know, I mean, who cares right now? Yeah, maybe I get a bit unlucky with the net cord. Who knows? Seriously, at this point I don't care anymore. It's all in the past.

More Novak Memories!

2007 Estoril Open With Novak Djokovic

By Miguel Seabra

As the press office manager of the 2007 Estoril Open I was mostly interested in Novak Djokovic and Andy Murray's performances - on and off the court.

I had previously talked with both Novak and Andy – but in very different environments at Masters and Grand Slam events. In Estoril, on my turf, I might be able to catch those little peculiarities that would help me better figure out their personalities for a feature I would be writing for my magazine, ProTENIS.

Unfortunately, Murray's back wasn't fully healed, and the withdrawal by Murray prevented the tournament from having five Top 10 players for the first time in it's history. It also prevented me from writing that Young Blood piece I was planning, but in the end I was happy: I got to know Djokovic pretty well and the tournament had a great addition to a pretty distinguished gallery of champions.

I must confess that, until the Australian Open of 2007, I didn't think the world of Djokovic. I viewed him as an inconsiderate iconoclast: too much talking, not enough results against top players. I was completely wrong. The kid has been dealing darn well with the spotlight and he was simply the star of the Estoril Open from Day One, showing great respect and manners.

Novak arrived in Portugal the Saturday before the main draw. And the first thing he asked me for was tickets to the big game the following day between Lisbon soccer giants Benfica and Sporting – a crucial match that could decide which team would follow runaway leader FC Porto into the Champions League next season. I told him that, at the time of the match the next day, he was supposed to attend the official players' dinner and party – and I was surprised by his reaction: "Well, if it's mandatory I should go to the dinner then."

Being ATP No. 5 in the world and a rising star crazy about soccer, Djokovic could do pretty much whatever he wanted, so his responsible reaction was surprising. Anyway, I still called João Lagos. I told him about my conversation with Novak. Lagos got right on the phone with Benfica's president and a little while later one of the club's directors called me, with some exciting news.

I went out to find Novak, who was practicing with his coach Marian Vajda, a stocky but smooth Slovak who got to the Estoril semifinals back in 1991. I was struck by how happy Djokovic appeared during his practice session, in fact, it was probably the most joyful practice session I can remember ever watching. The workout finished in gales of laughter when, in the last point of a mini-tennis match, Novak deftly faked out Vajda so badly that the coach fell on his back and ended up caked in red clay.

When they were done, I told Novak the good news: "Novak, the stadium is sold out, tomorrow night. Sorry. But . . .we've got four invitations to the presidential box."

The guy was ecstatic. The following day, we sat together in the first row of the exclusive box, alongside the usual assortment of ministers and diplomats and other VIPs. The match ended up a 1-1 tie, much to the dismay of Benfica supporters. The next morning, Benfica sent a present for Novak: an official team shirt with his name and favorite number (4) on the back. I went over to the players lounge and, with Marian Vajda and Novak's trainer, Ronen Bega, hung the red shirt on a nearby coat hook. When Novak joined us, he glanced it. A few moments later, he realized what it was, and that it was for him. He reacted like a kid on Christmas day.

I told Novak he could wear the shirt on court, before or after the match – since it was from his own sponsor, Adidas, it wouldn't be a problem for him, and his picture would be everywhere. A couple of hours later, I saw him heading to the stadium with Igor Andreev. The red Benfica jersey was nowhere to be seen. But right before walking on court, he stopped, took the shirt out of his bag, and put it on. The crowd in the stadium was sparse - he was first on, and it was lunch time - and they greeted him with a chorus of boos! I felt terrible, I should have realized the sociological realities at play: Benfica is the popular club, but tennis attracts a posh crowd, and they're largely Sporting supporters.

Novak took it in stride, though, and he broke Igor Andreev right at the beginning of the match. We couldn't forsee it, but from that break on until he clinched championship point, Novak performed like a veteran warrior. The conditions became - and stayed - extremely difficult. The wind was terrible, and it kept changing and swirling in different, unpredictable directions.

Igor Andreev, the the time the last man on the planet to beat Rafa Nadal on clay, was getting back to form after a lengthy injury and, with his big, high-bouncing, "Made in Spain" topspin forehand (Andreev left Moscow while in his teens), he soon started dictating play. Nole hung tough, but expressed frustration over not being able to play more aggressively. He was a break down in the third and the match was decided by a couple of points in the tiebreak: leading 3-2, Andreev double-faulted and then Novak finished off a long, intense exchange with a drop volley. He grabbed the momentum right there and went on to win the match and celebrated as if he'd won the whole tournament.

And then... he put on the Benfica jersey again and waved. He was booed a bit more than cheered, and on his way out he gestured to his ear and looked at me, a bit puzzled – but Vajda told him not to worry, that he did OK -it's just that it was a Sporting crowd. One person who did appreciate Novak's support was the Benfica striker, Italy's Fabrizio Miccoli. He was there, and he signed the shirt in a photo-op that was all over the papers the following day.

Novak addressed the shirt incident at the press conference with a lot of maturity and diplomacy. He is great in pressers, he talks clearly and frankly and interacts with the reporters as well as he does with the public. The kid's got charisma, no doubt about that. And a lot of people were happy to see him survive the stern test.

Novak's second rounder against Spain's Santiago Ventura was a mere formality and then things got complicated again in the quarters against Spanish shotmaker Guillermo Garcia-Lopez. The Djoker won the first set, then took a mental break in the second; he tried to regroup in the beginning of the third, but it wasn't easy with the wind blowing again – after a couple of demanding points, the combination of anxiety and eagerness got the best of him. Novak started having problems breathing.

With Garcia-Lopez leading, 2-1, Novak called for the trainer, who subsequently worked a little on Novak's back, too. The timing of that interruption was such that Garcia-Lopez later said, rather cryptically, that, "Novak is a very intelligent player." But the real difference is that, from 5-all onward, Novak simply was the tougher, more determined player.

In the semifinals, Tommy Robredo was 5-3 ahead and ultimately served for the first set, but Djokovic battled his way out of trouble yet again; the wind got to Robredo, and Djokovic won the first and then ran away with the second set.

The final was a bit of a roller coaster ride in front of a sellout crowd, with the sun shining high. But the wind was a disruptive factor again. The first set was a tight affair, with two breaks each, and Novak called for the trainer twice - he even got some eye drops because of the clay dust. And right there, at crunch time, everybody could see why Gasquet is No. 15 and Djokovic is 5: the Frenchman has flair, but he blew six set-points from 5-4 on due to some poor decisions, while his Serbian opponent made the most of his first set point, closing it out, 9-7.

Novak got broken in the first game of the second, then threw the racquet so hard you could hear it crack. He didn't get a warning, but from then, even the most diehard Djokovic fan had to admit that he appeared to tank. The way he let go that second set was dangerous, because he was clearly letting Richard back into the match, but he showed the confidence and Wilanders to get the momentum back exactly when he most needed it. Novak flicked the "on" switch again at the start of the third set, and raced to a 6-1 win.

Once again, I saw the good-humored, talkative kid whom I'd encountered at that first practice session of the tournament. Novak stripped and sent a racquet and his yellow shirt to the crowd. Then grabbed a red shirt from his bag – the crowd thought it was a Benfica jersey again, so a few started whistling. . .but Novak showed them it was Serbia's national team soccer shirt, with the embroidery proclaiming 'Made in Serbia' and 'Nole'. He got the trophy from Benfica legend Eusebio and then rushed like a kid to his bag to get the Benfica shirt. He asked Eusebio for an autograph in front of a packed stadium.

At the end of the trophy presentation I walked out to conduct the on-court interview. Novak acknowledged Eusebio and thanked everybody else, charming the crowd. My second question in the center court interview was: "None other than former great John McEnroe was quoted recently as saying that you are the best one of the new generation – that you are 'da man.' What do you think about that? And are you really da man?"
He was quick on his feet: "Obviously, everybody can see that I'm not a woman!"

The stadium erupted in laughter. He went on to say he was honored to hear that, etc. etc. I had thought before the tournament that he lacked a proper respect toward the game and his peers, but he showed nothing but class throughout.

After his official ATP mass press conference we finally had time to sit quietly over lunch and discuss several issues. Here are some of the things Novak said:

Tanking the second set in the Estoril Open final: Under those conditions, I need to be so much more focused. The people that understand me the most are the players who play at this level. I was really frustrated because I've played all matches in this tournament under difficult windy conditions, I needed a kind of a mental break and it's another lesson I need to learn – it shouldn't happen in the future. It's a professional sport, at this level you can't just give the opportunity to players like Gasquet because they're going to use it and then it's tough to come back. I was lucky to play better in the first game of the third set. I was kind of saving energy; you have to variate and compromise with everything.

On 'Dominating' Nadal at Roland Garros in 2006: I say what I feel. I try to be as nice as possible, but I felt in that match against Nadal I was the one giving away the points and making the points. Of course he's the best player in the surface, but what I was trying to explain the people is that I am an aggressive type of player and felt he wasn't questioned in the match and I was giving him the points. People got me wrong.

Before Federer match in Australia 2007: I didn't say 'he is going down.' What I said was that I'm going to try to win, I'm not going on court with a white flag. That's what I said, and I say what I think. I said it in a good way, but they thought I was arrogant, cocky, blah blah blah... well, you have to accept it is a part of our professional life... the press is the one that can rise you to the stars and then kill you in the same moment.

About medical time-outs in matches: Take the statistics... in five matches I retired, I was leading in four, the only one I was losing was that one against Nadal. Federer said everybody was pissed at me after that Davis Cup match last year in Geneva because I took a time out, but I was leading 2-0 in the fifth set. But they said whenever I'm losing I ask for a medical time-out. When I ask a medical time-out I'm not trying to confuse my opponent, I'm just trying to recover, to get ready. But people get me wrong.

McEnroe helping him: I try to improve my game, especially on the serve and the volley, getting more agressive to use my opportunities and Mark Woodforde helped me out a lot at Indian Wells and Miami. Of course John McEnroe had great volleys, great feeling, good serve – he's saying good things about me and it's another positive thought and another step towards a future cooperation. I'm trying to get a big team so I can improve my game and get my game together in order to make it perfect. You have to invest yourself. If you don't take the risks, you don't get the rewards.

Favorite play: It's a secret... but, as a young kid and throughout my career, I always liked the backhand down the line because it is a shot that changes something in the rally. I can do it, but I should do it more often.

What sets him apart from the others: I'm different from other players because I'm always trying to learn something new and trying to improve. Most other players don't do that, they stick to their games. Roger Federer is one that is trying to improve all the time. I'm always trying to get together those small things that I still miss.

Of course, I also had a chat with Marian Vajda: The Estoril Open was probably his most difficult title, considering the tough playing conditions. What I like the most about Novak is his winning attitude, he's one of the best fighters on the Tour and he likes to play matches, to compete. And he has very good skills. We're working on the approach and the net game, and still working on the serve, but we try to improve on a daily basis, step by step. He has a very powerful game, he can increase the level of the speed of the ball and change the pace in a match and not a lot of players can do that. His movement was always very good, but now he is more powerful in his upper body. And he is intelligent, likes to work and learns fast. I admire him a lot.

Then I asked him about McEnroe: Novak's father would like John to help him with the net game, and I think it's great, I'm OK with it.

In my conversation with Nole, it really struck me when he said: "I try to do everything with a smile and positive energy."

I knew that Novak uses a yellow Smiley-face string dampener, so I pulled out a copy of my magazine, in which I used a Smiley-face icon as a substitute for the letter "O" in the headline, The Djoker. He loved it; I told him since he always has the Smiley on his strings he should make it his trademark logo and capitalize on it because strong icons make names stronger – Bjorn Borg had the Bj logo, Seve Ballesteros has the silhouette of him winning at St. Andrews as a logo, the Rolling Stones have that iconic tongue...

I bid my goodbyes to Novak and his team and headed back to the press office. My mental image of him was that of the Smiley-face icon. I realized I was smiling, too, and the only thing that made me stop was remembering that I had meant to ask him for an autographed shirt (one of his own Adidas tennis numbers) to donate to the readers of TennisWorld, following a drawing or contest of some kind.

Miguel Seabra (Eurosport Comentator): Once we were going alongside a mirror and he looked at his image and said, 'I look like Brad Pitt... ... after a car crash.'

It was in Lisbon, Portugal, on our way back from soccer match (Lisbon Derby between Benfica and Sporting). I mean, how can you be arrogant - people say he is - if you say something like that?!?

Dr. Aaron Friedrich: I've encountered him many times at US Open qualies, Miami Open and at our hotel in Rome. He is a terrific guy, always friendly. Our best Novak story... The hotel in Rome has its own clay tennis court and one day I decided to go out and hit with my 10-year-old son. When we arrived to the court, who do we see exiting but none other than Novak Djokovic. There was no one else near him. I introduced myself and my son to him and he could not have been nicer as he posed for a photo with my 10-year-old side-by-side with their rackets. The only thing missing was my son getting a chance to rally with the Joker but maybe that will happen next time! To think we played on the court immediately after one of the greatest players of all time. That is a once-in-a-lifetime treat.

Never confuse faith you will prevail in the end - which you can never afford to lose - with the discipline to confront the most brutal facts of your current reality whatever they might be. - James Stockdale

No man is more unhappy than he who never faces adversity. For he is not permitted to prove himself. - Seneca

My Novak Djokovic Biofile
Interview at US Open

By Scoop Malinowski

Ht: 6-2 Wt: 176

DOB: May 22 1987 In: Belgrade Serbia

(Note: This interview with an eighteen year old Djokovic was done at the US Open in 2005 after his first round, five-set duel with Gael Monfils)

Tennis Heroes: "Well, Pete Sampras, he was always my idol. I always liked his game even if I don't have the same game as he does. I liked his attitude and the way he played. The way he act on the court I like a lot. He was concentrated a lot during all the matches. And he was playing the best tennis on the very important points, during the very important matches. That's what I liked about Pete Sampras. That's why he was always my idol. He finished his tennis career - I'm really sorry that I didn't have a chance to meet him and to play with him. But I hope in the next two years I will have a chance to meet him. And since he finished the tennis, I like a lot Federer's game and Safin. Safin actually played, not same, but similar game to mine - very aggressive and using all the opportunities. I had the chance to play against Safin in Australian Open and it was a great moment and a great experience, my first appearance on the big center court."

Tennis Inspirations: "A win. The feeling of winning a match or winning a tournament. The feeling of winning a tennis match is irreplaceable."

Favorite Movies: "Yeah, I'm a movie watcher. I like all kinds of movies, action and thrillers, drama and horror. The favorite one - maybe Pulp Fiction is one of the best."

Musical Tastes: "I'm a music fan also like everybody. For me, it is also important the company you have. When you are going out, company that's around you, then you don't really pay attention to music so much. I like R&B, house music, I don't like actually Serbian music, our music, so I'm not a big fan of this. So I'm listening to American, R&B, hip-hop, reggae, house. I like all kinds. Also classical sometimes when I need to relax."

Favorite Meal: "As a tennis player I have to eat a lot because I expend a lot of energy. Mostly during the day I'm eating pasta. So this is one of my favorite meals. But I also like a lot of chicken with mashed potatoes, and some salad.

That's like my favorite [laughs]."

Favorite Ice Cream Flavor: "Well, I like a lot of chocolate. I have to admit that. I like sweets a lot. So I like chocolate ice cream."

First Tennis Memory: "Yeah sure, I remember I started when I was four. My father owns a restaurant in one mountain in our country. And when I was four they were making three tennis courts in front of my restaurant. And I was helping them to make these courts. And I was interested a lot because no one in my family ever played tennis. My father was a professional skier. My mother was also skiing. And he also played soccer and wallyball, a lot of different sports, but not tennis. So I was the first to start playing tennis when I was four. The first coach, Jelena Gencic, she teach me how to play tennis and how to act on the court. She teach me a lot. This was very important to have a good coach in the period when I was seven years old to eleven. And I was really lucky to have her."

Pre-Match Feeling: "Well, I try not to think too much because I want to be focused for the match. Before the match I do the usual warmup, stretching. I need 30-45 minutes to prepare all my racquets and everything. I'm thinking... mostly I'm speaking with my coach about what tactics we should prepare for this player. Think tactics, strategy, how I should act on the court, what should I use more. These kinds of things. I try not to think too much. I just go out on the court and do my best."

Greatest Sports Moment: "I have a few moments that I like. At Wimbledon when I reached the third round in 2005 was really great. In second round I saved five match points from 0-2, I came to 3-2 to win. This was a great moment. And this was really important match for me. Because when I won the match I got to top 100. So this was really nice feeling. And also the fact that I played the first time on the grass. So that's really nice, I like Wimbledon a lot."

Most Painful Moment: "Well, I cannot say that I really had a painful tennis moment that I wanted to quit tennis or something like that. I hope that I will not have. Probably being injured or not feeling 100% healthy. But I never had any really like painful moments."

Favorite Tournaments: "I like Australia and Wimbledon a lot. I like the Grand Slams."

Funny Tennis Memory: "I like to watch McEnroe playing. He was really funny on the court. And Safin, when he would throw the racquet when he was really nervous. And it was really fun watching Yannick Noah. I like watching the old matches when I was really a baby. And McEnroe was really funny."

Embarrassing Tennis Memory: "Well, when I lost to one guy from Serbia actually. It was about seven or eight years ago when I was first in Europe. I lost to this guy and it was really embarrassing because everybody expected me to win easily, so."

Closest Tennis Friends: "I'm really in good relationship with everybody. So I'm trying to keep it that way. I'm really good friends with Janko Tipsarevic and the players from my country."

Funniest Players Encountered: "I don't know. Everybody is funny. I don't put out one."

Toughest Competitors Encountered: "Well, all the players are tough to play against, everybody is trying their best to win the match."

People Qualities Most Admired: "Just I like people who have a lot of sense of humor. And who are very honest. I like nice people, like really honest person, who can be good friends of yours. It's really difficult because every where you go you meet a lot of people and it's difficult to find your friend. Like real honest friends."

You can read more of Scoop's Biofile interviews at **www.mrbiofile.com**

Novak Djokovic Facts & Records

Won 20 Grand Slams - 9 Australian Open, 6 Wimbledon, 2 Roland Garros, 3 US Open.

First ATP singles title was Dutch Open in Amersfoort 2006.

First and only ATP doubles title was in Queens Club with Jonathan Erlich in 2010.

Played in 31 Grand Slam singles finals.

Won 86 ATP singles titles.

Finishes as ATP Year End No. 1 seven times - 2011, 2012, 2014, 2015, 2018, 2020, 2021.

Only man to win every major ATP Masters and ATP Finals at least twice.

Only man along with Roy Emerson and Rod Laver to win all four Grand Slams twice.

Won 37 Masters singles titles.

Most weeks ranked No. 1.

Only man to win 6 Masters titles in one year (2015).

Only man to play in 8 Masters finals in one year (2015).

Won a record 31 Masters consecutive matches.

Novak Djokovic Quotes

2007 Rome

I always learn some new things when I play against the best players in the world. Every match is a new experience. I'm not really in a hurry anywhere. I'm trying to practice and to focus on my career. And I know that I need a lot of experience and a lot of things to improve on so I can get to the place I want to be: The best player in the world.

There is time. I'm only twenty years old this year. I hope my career will be ten to fifteen more years long. What I will try to do is to improve more on the volleys so I can use my opportunities. Because I have pretty good groundstrokes from the baseline, pretty powerful and aggressive, but I need to go more to the net so I can use those opportunities, and of course serve consistency.

There is a lot of things. You cannot play perfect. There is always things you can improve on.

2007 Wimbledon

Why should I be frightened (to say I can beat Federer)? For me it's totally normal thing. If you go out on the court thinking positively and thinking, I can win against anybody, I think that's a right thinking. If you go with the white flag on the court, what you're doing there? You know what I mean?

Federer is surely No. 1 player of the world already for last four years, the best player, most consistent player, probably one of the best tennis players in the history of this sport. We all know that.

But looking from my point of view I really want to get to that place. That's my goal: To be No. 1 player of the world. I'm really going slowly even though I made fantastic results in last two years. But I'm really trying to go step by step, really slowly, and I'm sure that my time will come.

Even though I lost four times to him, I'm still working on my strokes, on my game. Every time I play him or Nadal I learn something new and see the things, negative things, what I need to improve on so I can win next time.

2008 Australian Open

I always believed. You know, I always believed. I didn't want to think in a negative way. I always had a big support, especially from my parents, my father. I think he always believed more in me than I did in myself.

With the way I was playing throughout all the junior years and junior events, I think I earned enough confidence and motivation to be a professional tennis player and to be as a Grand Slam champion.

2010 US Open

As I said on the post-match interview, it's one of those matches that you will remember for the rest of your life, not just because you won against one of the best players that ever played this game (Federer) at that occasion, but as well, you know, coming back from match points down and under the circumstances playing good tennis and winning in the end, the thriller. So I am. I am very proud of myself. There are a lot of emotions involved. Of course I was too exhausted to show them in the end. But it's been a fantastic semifinal.

2011 Wimbledon

We all know the careers of Nadal and Federer. We don't need to spend words again. They have been the two most dominant players in the world the last five years. They have won most of the majors we are playing in. So sometimes it did feel a little bit frustrating when you kind of get to the later stages of a Grand Slam, meaning last four, last eight, and then you have to meet them. They always come up with their best tennis when it matters the most.

But, look, it's a process of learning, a process of developing and improving as a tennis player, as a person, and just finding the way to mentally overcome those pressures and expectations and issues that you have.

I always believed that I have quality to beat those two guys. I always believed I have quality to win majors, Grand Slams, and that was the only way I could be here in this position.

I have full respect for those two guys, what they have done. Anytime I play them, it's a great match. But the mental approach has to be positive. I have to win this match. There's no other way.

2012 US Open

Andy has all the capacity he needs, all the talent on the court. He's dedicated, he's professional. He has proven that many years already, with his results. Us four, we are taking this game to another level, and it's really nice to be part of such a strong men's tennis era.

2013 Wimbledon

Wimbledon was without a doubt always a tournament that I wanted to win, that I dreamed of winning, that I visualized holding this trophy when I was only six, seven years old.

When I won it back in 2011 it was definitely the highlight of my career, and it still is. I went back and shared that trophy with my dearest ones in my life, all my family, friends, all the people who have participated in my life in some way. One of the most important people was Jelena Gencic. I was very happy to bring the trophy back to her at her home. We had a little celebration.

Of course, going back to Belgrade, being welcomed by 100,000 people on the main square, was something that will probably never happen again. It's the most beautiful experience I had as a person, as an athlete. It was unbelievable.

I never, never expected that something like that can happen. It meant a lot not just to me but to whole nation. Wimbledon is, as it shows, the biggest tournament in sport. It's why people pay a lot of attention to what's going on here.

Andres Bella Art.

2015 US Open

I'm a different player, a different person today than I was 2011. As a father and a husband, experiencing different variety of things in my life, it's completely different approach to tennis today. I feel more fulfilled. I feel more complete as a player today than I was in 2011. Physically stronger, mentally more experienced, and tougher, as well. Trying to use the experience from before into every match that I play, and especially the big ones like today.

The season is not over, but the Grand Slam is over. The biggest tournaments that I have played this year, as anybody else, and I won three out of four. It's more than I could ask for, definitely. Of course I do have lots of expectations and high ambitions whenever I'm approaching the Grand Slams or any other tournament, but now actually sitting down here with this trophy and reflecting on what I have achieved, it's quite incredible.

So I'm definitely very satisfied and proud of that. As you said, he played great tennis throughout the entire year. I think as the season was going by he was elevating his game. He was improving. Now he came up with a different shot, as well, the shot that nobody has ever seen. And it's been working well also against me in Cincinnati and also here. He's just not going away. He's not dropping his level too much. I was saying on the court that he's always going to be out there making you play your best if you want to win.

So that's who Roger is. That's why he has won so many Grand Slam titles. And I knew that coming to the court. I knew he's going to be aggressive. He's going to try to disrupt my rhythm, and he's going to put a lot of variety in his game. slice, chip and charge, come to the net, serve and volley. Which he did.

But I was ready for it. I was ready for the battle. That's what it was. Three hours, 20 minutes. We pushed each other to the limit, as we always do. It's an ultimate challenge that I can have now winning against Roger back to back finals in Wimbledon and here, US Open. It's tremendous. I'm really, really proud of it.

2018 Cincinnati

First and only player to win all nine Masters 1000 titles...

Definitely one of the most special moments in my career. Achievements, making history of the sport that I truly love is a great privilege and honor and something that I'll be very proud of for the rest of my life. I was saying previously that during this week that obviously this trophy has been a motivation, big motivation for me. But at the same time I tried not to think about the pressure of really making history too much, because I have had already some failed attempts, three years ago with Roger, and coming into today's match, I mean, wasn't easy psychologically because I knew I lost to him every time I played him on this court. But at the same time, I liked my chances because I felt better and better as the tournament week was progressing. I felt that in the past when I had this particular circumstances in the tournament and matches where I come back from situations where I'm down a set and a break and I managed to win close matches, I usually come out semifinals or finals playing my best tennis. That's something that I was hoping is going to happen again, and I believed that it will and it did. It was by far the best performance of the week.

I said on the court, it's a pleasure to share the court with him, with the all-time great, I truly mean that. With him, with Nadal, these guys have been such an integral, important part of my life and my career and my evolution as a tennis player. They make me play my best tennis. They make me improve. They made me think about what I need to do in order to try to be the best player in the world.

2019 Wimbledon

Well, it was a huge relief in the end, honestly. In these kind of matches, you work for, you live for, they give sense and they give value to every minute you spend on the court training and working to get yourself in this position and play the match with one of your greatest rivals of all time. That was one thing that I promised myself coming on to the court today, that I need to stay calm and composed, because I knew that the atmosphere will be as it was.

Obviously Roger is playing well. I kind of predicted the scenarios in my head already, visualized what's going to happen. It was probably the most demanding, mentally most demanding, match I was ever part of. I had the most physically demanding match against Nadal in the finals of Australia that went almost six hours. But mentally this was different level, because of everything.

I'm just obviously thrilled and overjoyed with emotions to be sitting here in front of you as a winner. It was one shot away from losing the match, as well. This match had everything. It could have gone easily his way. He was serving extremely well, I thought, the entire match. I had a lot of difficulties to read his serve. Well, it was kind of a flashback of US Open when I saved the two match points against him, as well.

But look, in these kind of moments, I just try to never lose self-belief, just stay calm, just focus on trying to get the ball back, return, which wasn't serving me very well today. But in the most important moments, all three tiebreaks I guess, if I can say so, I found my best game.

2021 US Open

So many different emotions. What I said on the ceremony, I really mean it. Of course, part of me is very sad. It's a tough one to swallow, this loss, I mean, considering everything that was on the line. But on the other hand I felt something I never felt in my life here in New York. The crowd made me very special. They pleasantly surprised me. I did not know, I did not expect anything, but the amount of support and energy and love I got from the crowd was something that I'll remember forever. I mean, that's the reason on the changeover I just teared up. The emotion, the energy was so strong. I mean, it's as strong as winning 21 Grand Slams. That's how I felt, honestly. I felt very, very special.

They touched my heart, honestly. Of course, in the end of the day you want to win. You're a professional athlete. These are the kind of moments that you cherish. These are connections that you establish with people that will be lasting for a very long time. Yeah, it was just wonderful.

January 7, 2022

The Hypocrisy Of Demonizing Novak Djokovic

When a true genius appears in the world,
you may know him by this sign: that the dunces are
all in confederacy against him. - Jonathan Swift

By Scoop Malinowski

Bradenton, FL - The world is so upside down today, Novak Djokovic has been portrayed by the world media essentially as a criminal because he stands firm on his personal principle of refusing to be injected by a vaccine drug shot that is a proven failure.

The establishment and world media have conspired to demonize Novak Djokovic as some kind of terrible villain. But remember what Malcolm X said about the media: "The media has the power to make the innocent look guilty and the guilty look innocent."

Djokovic followed all the protocols in Australia, even got a note from AO tournament director about steps he should follow to compete/defend his title as a non vaccinated player, just like some of the other players who will compete as anonymous non vax players.

But the world media lynch mob rabidly resents Djokovic's firm, strong, inspiring resistance to reject the drug shot and rely on his own natural immunity and healthy lifestyle to beat the covid virus or flu or whatever it really is who the hell knows for sure? Political weapon? Diabolical scheme to steal our freedoms? A toxic secret mark of the beast shot to alter our DNA and leave humanity open to be manipulated/controlled by AI intelligence? Anything is possible. Whatever happened to freedom of choice?

As the world media lynch mob and Covid tyranny establishment attack, maim, and demonize the greatest champion sports figure in the world today, let me remind you of some of the other famous criminals in tennis who somehow avoided being mercilessly attacked by the world media lynch mob.

This famous champion and TV commentator was accused by his movie star ex-wife of assaulting and abusing her in her book, she also alleged he is a massive drug addict.

This former champion once pushed a girlfriend out of a moving car and had a relationship with an underage girl, even bringing her to tournaments.

This current low ranked doubles competitor was caught with an underage girl at his hotel by the girl's father who rescued her from a sexual assault in Washington DC. This story never made the news.

This former loud mouthed bad boy from Eastern Europe has his name in Jeffrey Epstein's black book.

Do we even have to name all the Grand Slam champions who were either arrested with cocaine or who were admitted addicts?

How about the former world no. 1 who began a relationship with his future wife when she was an underaged minor.

Remember the wild woman who threatened to assault and kill a lineswoman and umpire because she disagreed with the calls made against her? The same tennis establishment still works overtime to protect her reputation and image because she's a political favorite despite her sometimes homicidal threatening behavior when enraged.

How about the famous former world no. 1 who snorted so many lines at a

Rush concert at Madison Square Garden the record label manager witness said he never saw any rock and roller in his life snort as much as he saw the tennis player snort that night.

How about the former no. 1 and four time Grand Slam winner and current TV analyst who was disqualified from the 1997 Monte Carlo Open after he cursed twice and then after losing a point, kicked the umpire's chair. The DQ cost the player nearly $20,000. The player and his partner were losing 1-4 in the third set to Luis Lobo and Javier Sanchez.

How about this same player who once hit an errant or targeted return at the chair umpire at the Miami Open, hitting the umpire in the leg. This was because he was angry about some line calls in a match with Pete Sampras, which he eventually lost.

How about the super agent of tennis who was called "evil" by a high school classmate: 'I know him from high school in Riverdale the Bronx. He bullied a kid. The student wasn't special ed. He was sort of an awkward, uncoordinated, unpopular, and frankly unattractive kid. Someone who didn't exactly need being knocked down a peg. (Name withheld), conversely, was the definitive Prom King type. He was a handsome kid, big for his age, popular and a tremendous athlete. There was zero justification for him to go after this other harmless kid. And yet he gave him the name "Ugly." He didn't call him by his name which was Todd. Always just called him Ugly. "Hey, Ugly." (Name withheld) was basically a Nazi. I don't think it is hyperbolic for me to call that evil. This kid was harmless. Not a wise ass.'

You probably don't know any of these scandalous tales... but you do know about the world champion who refuses to take the drug shot which has been a proven failure. And you probably believe, because of heavy media manipulation wanting you to believe that he is the worst villain in tennis history.

But the reality is Novak Djokovic may be the most courageous, principled, heroic champion in the history of any sport.

About The Author

 **Mark "Scoop" Malinowski** was born in Philadelphia, PA and first attended the US Open in 1989 and watched Ivan Lendl beat 19-year-old Jim Courier 61 62 63 in the third round on Louie Armstrong Stadium and McEnroe/Woodforde defeat Evernden/Steeb 63 63 on the old grandstand in doubles with Tatum O'Neal sitting just a few seats away.

By 1992 Scoop started a Biofile interview column in the Morristown Daily Record and attended the Pathmark Classic in Mahwah, NJ which featured Monica Seles. Thirty years later he's authored twelve tennis books and has written about tennis for Final Magazine, Tennis Magazine, Tennis Week Magazine, Ace Magazine, ATPworldtour.com, Australian Tennis Magazine and many other publications.

Some of the tennis champions he has done Biofile interviews with include Margaret Court, Don Budge, Pete Sampras, Roger Federer, Rafael Nadal, Jimmy Connors, Billie Jean King, Chris Evert, Mats Wilander, Guillermo Vilas, Andres Gomez, Ivan Lendl, Fred Stolle, John Newcombe, Jim Courier, Yevgeny Kafelnikov, Stan Wawrinka, Martina Hingis, Venus Williams, Maria Bueno, Virginia Wade, Virginia Ruzici, Michael Chang, Marat Safin, Andy Murray, Juan Martin Del Potro, Gustavo Kuerten, Goran Ivanisevic, Sergi Bruguera, John McEnroe, Roy Emerson, Jack Kramer, Petr Korda, Gaston Gaudio, Marin Cilic, Patrick Rafter, Carlos Moya, Stefan Edberg, Ana Ivanovic, Vika Azarenka, Flavia Pennetta, Francesca Schiavone, Ash Barty, Mary Pierce, Manuel Santana, Juan Carlos Ferrero, Johan Kriek, Roscoe Tanner, Arthur Ashe, Andy Roddick, Stan Smith, Richard Krajicek, Pat Cash, Marion Bartoli, Sam Stosur, Conchita Martinez, Barbora Krejcikova, Simona Halep.

Thanks to Miguel Seabra, Aaron Friedrich, Andres Bella, Henk Abbink, Alberto Ramirez Saurez for photographs and artwork. Special thanks to all the players, media, fans who cooperated with this project; the ATP World Tour, ASAP Sports, Miami Open, Newport Hall of Fame Championships, Sarasota Open Challenger, Tallahassee Challenger.

Scoop Malinowski's Books

> Facing Federer

> Facing Nadal

> Facing McEnroe

> Facing Andy Murray

> Facing Hewitt

> Facing Sampras

> Facing Marat Safin

> Facing Serena Williams/Steffi Graf (Double book)

> Close Encounters With Donald Trump

> The Book Of Joy

> Facing Guillermo Vilas

> Marcelo Rios: The Man We Barely Knew

> Muhammad Ali: Portrait of a Champion

> Heavyweight Armageddon: The Tyson vs Lewis Heavyweight Championship Battle

> Facing Bob Probert

> 80's Hockey Biofiles

> Facing Bjorn Borg

You can read Scoop's tennis coverage at www.tennis-prose.com.

Printed in Great Britain
by Amazon

35887976R00079